Forces Shaping Community College Missions

Kristin Bailey Wilson
Regina L. Garza Mitchell
EDITORS

Number 180 • Winter 2017
Jossey-Bass
San Francisco

Forces Shaping Community College Missions
Kristin Bailey Wilson and Regina L. Garza Mitchell (eds.)
New Directions for Community Colleges, no. 180

Editor-in-Chief: *Arthur M. Cohen*
Associate Editors: *Caroline Q. Durdella, Nathan R. Durdella*
Managing Editor: *Amy Fara Edwards*

New Directions for Community Colleges, (ISSN 0194-3081; Online ISSN: 1536-0733), is published quarterly by Wiley Subscription Services, Inc., a Wiley Company, 111 River St., Hoboken, NJ 07030-5774 USA.

Postmaster: Send all address changes to *New Directions for Community Colleges*, John Wiley & Sons Inc., C/O The Sheridan Press, PO Box 465, Hanover, PA 17331 USA.

Information for subscribers

New Directions for Community Colleges is published in 4 issues per year. Institutional subscription prices for 2017 are:

Print & Online: US$454 (US), US$507 (Canada & Mexico), US$554 (Rest of World), €363 (Europe), £285 (UK). Prices are exclusive of tax. Asia-Pacific GST, Canadian GST/HST and European VAT will be applied at the appropriate rates. For more information on current tax rates, please go to www.wileyonlinelibrary.com/tax-vat. The price includes online access to the current and all online back files to January 1st 2013, where available. For other pricing options, including access information and terms and conditions, please visit www.wileyonlinelibrary.com/access.

Delivery Terms and Legal Title

Where the subscription price includes print issues and delivery is to the recipient's address, delivery terms are **Delivered at Place (DAP)**; the recipient is responsible for paying any import duty or taxes. Title to all issues transfers FOB our shipping point, freight prepaid. We will endeavour to fulfil claims for missing or damaged copies within six months of publication, within our reasonable discretion and subject to availability.

Back issues: Single issues from current and recent volumes are available at the current single issue price from cs-journals@wiley.com.

Disclaimer

The Publisher and Editors cannot be held responsible for errors or any consequences arising from the use of information contained in this journal; the views and opinions expressed do not necessarily reflect those of the Publisher and Editors, neither does the publication of advertisements constitute any endorsement by the Publisher and Editors of the products advertised.

Publisher: New Directions for Community Colleges is published by Wiley Periodicals, Inc., 350 Main St., Malden, MA 02148–5020.

Journal Customer Services: For ordering information, claims and any enquiry concerning your journal subscription please go to www.wileycustomerhelp.com/ask or contact your nearest office.
Americas: Email: cs-journals@wiley.com; Tel: +1 781 388 8598 or +1 800 835 6770 (toll free in the USA & Canada).
Europe, Middle East and Africa: Email: cs-journals@wiley.com; Tel: +44 (0) 1865 778315.
Asia Pacific: Email: cs-journals@wiley.com; Tel: +65 6511 8000.
Japan: For Japanese speaking support, Email: cs-japan@wiley.com.
Visit our Online Customer Help available in 7 languages at www.wileycustomerhelp.com/ask

Production Editor: Shreya Srivastava (email: shsrivsata@wiley.com).

Wiley's Corporate Citizenship initiative seeks to address the environmental, social, economic, and ethical challenges faced in our business and which are important to our diverse stakeholder groups. Since launching the initiative, we have focused on sharing our content with those in need, enhancing community philanthropy, reducing our carbon impact, creating global guidelines and best practices for paper use, establishing a vendor code of ethics, and engaging our colleagues and other stakeholders in our efforts. Follow our progress at www.wiley.com/go/citizenship

View this journal online at wileyonlinelibrary.com/journal/cc

Wiley is a founding member of the UN-backed HINARI, AGORA, and OARE initiatives. They are now collectively known as Research4Life, making online scientific content available free or at nominal cost to researchers in developing countries. Please visit Wiley's Content Access – Corporate Citizenship site: http://www.wiley.com/WileyCDA/Section/id-390082.html

Printed in the USA by The Sheridan Group.

Address for Editorial Correspondence should be sent to the Editor-in-Chief, Arthur M. Cohen, at 1749 Mandeville Lane, Los Angeles, CA 90049. All manuscripts receive anonymous reviews by external referees.

Abstracting and Indexing Services

The Journal is indexed by Academic Search Alumni Edition (EBSCO Publishing); Education Index/Abstracts (EBSCO Publishing); ERA: Educational Research Abstracts Online (T&F); ERIC: Educational Resources Information Center (CSC); MLA International Bibliography (MLA).

Cover design: Wiley
Cover Images: © Lava 4 images | Shutterstock

For submission instructions, subscription and all other information visit:
wileyonlinelibrary.com/journal/cc

CONTENTS

Editors' Notes

Historically, community colleges have been identified as open-door institutions, their distinctiveness closely connected to ideas of educational opportunity and, by extension, democracy. The open door of the community college symbolizes the American ideal of opportunity—the opportunity to better oneself and one's social standing through access to a college education irrespective of educational background, household income, or demographic traits. Today, the community colleges remain the embodiment of educational democracy in the United States.

Yet, there is a disparity between the stated goals of the community colleges and the achievement of those goals; or rather, the degree to which the promise of the colleges is enacted. Transfer and graduation rates continue to be lower than we would like them to be, and students sometimes incur significant debt to attend these low-cost institutions. Community colleges have struggled to help students succeed in developmental course sequences and to transfer smoothly, without the loss of credits, to 4-year counterparts. Maintaining the currency of vocational curriculum is expensive and requires that faculty maintain close partnerships with industry.

In 2006, Townsend and Dougherty published a volume on community college missions. In their volume, they distinguished between societal missions and functional missions saying, "societal missions underlie functional missions" (p. 1). This is an easy notion to read but a more difficult one to apply. What societal mission underlies developmental education? Why are so many community college students stuck in the developmental sequence? If the societal mission is to offer basic education to those who did not receive one in high school, are community colleges succeeding at the functional work? Questions continue. Do all students need a background in algebra? Do all students need to write the classic academic essay? How does this work help the heating, ventilation, and air conditioning (HVAC) technician? Although we in education know the philosophical and practical answers, the dropout rate from developmental courses and the developmental sequence offers a painful response from one stakeholder group: students—leading us back to the relationship between societal missions and functional missions. Who determines them and how will they be accomplished? We do not definitively answer any of these questions in this volume, but we seek to offer a thoughtful treatment of how community college leaders might think about the tensions from practitioner and scholar viewpoints. This volume

New Directions for Community Colleges, no. 180, Winter 2017 © 2017 Wiley Periodicals, Inc.
Published online in Wiley Online Library (wileyonlinelibrary.com) • DOI: 10.1002/cc.20275

revisits the topic of mission and demonstrates the evolving nature of the multiple missions of community college.

In Chapter 1, Ayers considers the history of the mission statement and the purposes mission statements serve for community colleges. He argues that these statements serve to remind the college and its constituents of the college mission even as the environment becomes increasingly unstable.

The idea of higher education having an unspoken social contract is not new. Heelan and Mellow view the social contract as a means of promoting and maintaining equity in the colleges' local communities. Using their years of experience as community college presidents, they explore how the social contract drives the community college mission and provides recommendations for leading internally and externally in ways that promote the contract.

The earliest community colleges served recent high school graduates; however, with the end of World War II, the mission changed to include students returning to school after military service or years of work. In Chapter 3, Davidson describes the current context for adult basic education located at the community college and names what he believes are three nationwide shifts that will determine the future direction for adult education.

Transfer is a classic community college mission; Joliet Junior College, traditionally touted as the first community college, began as a transfer institution. Baldwin discusses contemporary mobility patterns and the ways policy both facilitates and impedes student transfer, the first community college mission.

In Chapter 5, D'Amico addresses the community aspect of mission by discussing the role of noncredit courses at community colleges. He focuses his attention on the ways noncredit work can respond to local needs quickly and effectively, and he names the ways community college leaders might take advantage of this nimble mission area to better respond to their communities.

Chapter 6, by Garza Mitchell and Sawyer, covers the role community colleges play in workforce development. The authors name many of the tensions and challenges community college leaders face as they seek to upgrade and develop workforce programs. Locating the funding to start expensive workforce programs in the current revenue context is certainly one of the more vexing challenges for leaders.

Increasing the number of Americans with college credentials is a state and national goal. Because community colleges offer an open door, many leaders view community colleges as central to improve completion rates. State merit scholarships based on minimal merit criteria are used to encourage college attendance by billing them as free community college. In Chapter 7, Buchanan and Wilson outline the free community college movement. The chapter includes many of the challenges community college leaders will face in states with policies offering "free" college. Is free community college an open door?

A growing aspect of the access mission is reaching out to a wider pool of students. As more and more state secondary systems are tying funding for high schools to postsecondary offerings in partnership with colleges, community colleges are being increasingly asked to offer dual credit classes. Jones' chapter discusses the ways dual credit classes can offer access that supports college completion.

Chapter 9, by Hellmich and Feeney, highlights how community college leaders can seek mission balance using strategic planning and clear-sighted decisions to accomplish goals. Finally, Amey sums up the work in the volume and offers encouragement to community college leaders seeking to make thoughtful, democratic, mission-focused decisions at their colleges.

There are some mission edges that we were not able to cover in this volume that are worth mentioning. What importance is being placed on internationalizing community college campuses by community college leaders? How is it being accomplished? How important is internationalizing curriculum to faculty and leaders? Are honors programs growing at community colleges? Do they meet regional needs? How? Should community colleges be the locations for small business incubators? Who should profit and how? Also, we have said too little about the reliance on adjunct labor and the quality of their work lives. We have not fully addressed the funding or revenue crisis at community colleges. In this volume, we have not given enough attention to the student services functions at community colleges. Finally, how will the growth of community college baccalaureate degree programs continue to shape the mission of community colleges? Nonetheless, the discussions about community college leadership throughout the volume offer ways to think about these mission edges and to grow missions within a context of revenue constraint.

Kristin Bailey Wilson
Regina L. Garza Mitchell
Editors

Reference

Townsend, B. K., & Dougherty, K. J. (2006). Editor's notes. In B. K. Townsend & K. J. Dougherty (Eds.), *Community college missions in the 21st century*, New Directions for Community Colleges: No. 136 (pp. 1–5). San Francisco, CA: Jossey-Bass.

KRISTIN BAILEY WILSON *is an associate professor in the department of Educational Administration, Leadership, and Research at Western Kentucky University.*

REGINA L. GARZA MITCHELL *is an associate professor of higher education leadership in the department of Educational Leadership, Research, and Technology at Western Michigan University.*

1

This chapter describes the historical context of community college mission statements and proposes that these texts serve three functions: public relations, management, and sensemaking.

Three Functions of the Community College Mission Statement

David F. Ayers

The junior college emerged at the turn of the twentieth century as a novel institution. Students, community leaders, state legislators, and the business community lacked the cognitive blueprints for this new institution type; no model existed in the public consciousness. It fell upon the leaders of the community college movement to establish a compelling institutional purpose—one that would both distinguish the junior college from other institutions and carry the new institution into the future. Just as important, early community college leaders had to communicate this purpose in ways that resonated with societal expectations. No single vision for the institution's future existed, and a politics of purpose ensued. For decades, community college leaders quarreled over what the institution should and could offer to its constituents.

Even as these quarrels played out, community college leaders faced immediate organizational challenges, not the least of which was to reconcile divergent societal demands (e.g., collegiate education versus vocational training) with diminishing resources. Leaders turned to various management practices to negotiate these challenges (Birnbaum, 2001). One management practice in particular gained traction: Drucker's (1973) concept of missioning. Community college leaders began to use the mission statement as a way to establish a collective sense of purpose and to guide planning.

The task of setting priorities became increasingly difficult as society became more complex. Community college educators had to make sense of pressing issues including, among others, globalization, inequality, technological revolution, and diminishing public investment. The mission statement—both as a text and a process—became one way for leaders make sense of a turbulent societal milieu and to anchor the college to a shared

NEW DIRECTIONS FOR COMMUNITY COLLEGES, no. 180, Winter 2017 © 2017 Wiley Periodicals, Inc.
Published online in Wiley Online Library (wileyonlinelibrary.com) • DOI: 10.1002/cc.20276

purpose in a sea change that otherwise would leave the organization hopelessly adrift.

Given this situation, the principal argument in this chapter is that the community college mission statement is used to accomplish three main tasks. First, the mission statement functions as a public relations document. It distinguishes the community college from other postsecondary institutions and garners the support of legislators, community members, and other constituents. Second, it serves a management function by guiding strategic planning and budgeting. Third, it functions in a constructive sense, both as sensemaking and as negotiation of competing interests internal and external to the college. These functions are not discrete but interrelated, although the relative degree of importance of each function may shift according to changes in the institutional environment. In what follows, I discuss the three functions of mission statements. First, however, I speculate about the origins of the mission statement within the community college context.

Origins of the Mission Statement

Community college leaders only began to use the mission statement in the second half of the twentieth century when Peter Drucker (1973) popularized the use of "missioning" as a management strategy. By the time, Drucker introduced "missioning" as a management strategy, the discourse of mission had been used within religious and military institutions for decades—even centuries. First, the term "mission" reflected the collective efforts of Christian missionaries on assignment. Whether it referred to sixteenth century Spanish missions in the Americas or the evangelical ventures of modern Christians, use of the term "mission" as an organized effort toward a specific outcome was well established within modern English lexicon. Second, the concept of mission was prominent within military contexts. For example, the mission as a collective purpose entered into the broader public conscience with the Apollo space missions. Similarly, the nose art on World War II aircraft was known as "mission symbols" (Apple, 2015). When a team of aviators destroyed an enemy target, they advanced the military mission and recorded their achievement as a "kill mark" near the cockpit of the aircraft. In 1946, the United States Educational Mission to Japan realized a joint mission involving both the military and educators. These education experts reported to General Douglas MacArthur to restructure the educational system of postwar Japan (Stoddard, 1946). This endeavor, quite possibly, facilitated the recontextualization (Fairclough, 2015) of a mission discourse within the practice of educational leadership.

Whether present in religious or military contexts, an organizational discourse of "mission" provided leaders with a mechanism for reducing a wide range of possible organizational actions to a manageable and measurable set of key priorities. With Drucker's work well received within management circles, missioning soon appeared within higher education contexts

(Keller, 1983). The community college context was fertile ground for this concept, and there was little delay in appropriating it (see also Birnbaum, 2001).

Today, the mission statement is a standard feature of contemporary organizations, including community colleges. After all, what legitimate community college does not have a mission statement? It has even become embedded in accreditation standards (Orwig & Finney, 2007). The Southern Association of Colleges and Schools (2012), for example, lists the following as a requirement for accreditation: "The institution has a clearly defined, comprehensive, and published mission statement that is specific to the institution and appropriate for higher education. The mission addresses teaching and learning and, where applicable, research and public service" (p. 18). Indeed, mission statements are ubiquitous in the organizational realm of contemporary society. At least for community colleges, the mission statement functions toward three ends. Each is discussed next.

Public Relations: Communicating the Purposes of a Novel Institution

In the first half of the twentieth century, when the community college movement accelerated, comparisons with secondary schools and collegiate institutions were inevitable. Early leaders needed to distinguish the junior college to garner public support: "When the public realizes the full significance of the junior-college movement, then—and only then—will we receive the maximum in cooperation and support" (McCoy, 1947, p. 1). To achieve this task, leaders of the community college movement circulated statements of institutional purpose in various print media.

One prominent genre was the junior college catalog. In 1930, Doak S. Campbell examined statements of purpose in 343 junior college catalogs. He tallied 783 "mentions" of specific purposes and organized these into four categories: preparatory, terminal and occupational, democratization, and popularizing higher education. Attempts to clarify institutional purpose also appeared in recruitment fliers, radio advertisements, and policy statements. Even still, community college leaders perhaps felt that such statements failed to capture the spirit of the community college movement:

> Each junior college has its traditional raison d'etre, its role to play, and its clientele to serve. ... These institutions ... have some avowed differences that are mythical and some that are real, although the real differences may in some cases be inconsequential. The individual junior college will and should have an individuality due to both nature and nurture: The conventional statement of objectives, curricula, and general information, as given in the annual bulletin or catalog, may not reveal some of the significant traits that make a junior college an institutional personality. (Chadwick, 1947, p. 305)

Thus even as the community college sought to establish a coherent institutional identity, there was a concern that statements of purpose failed to
represent the activities of local colleges.

Statements of institutional identity in print media also attempted to
inform potential students about the opportunities the junior college provided. Two examples follow. First, in 1952, Colorado public junior colleges
distributed a four-page brochure to all high school seniors in the state. It
urged students to "attend a junior college near your home—become a part
of the fastest growing educational movement in the United States of America" (American Association of Junior Colleges, 1952, p. 531). Second, in
1975, Eileen Kuhns (1974) reported on a conference of 100 educators who
considered policies and strategies to promote cross-institutional mobility
of transfer students. Among the recommendations was that administrators
"provide leadership in: (a) defining the institutional mission and depart-
mental and course objectives, and (b) accurately publicizing these in order
that potential students may be able to make well-informed choices about
the college and its offerings" (Kuhns, 1974, p. 16). In sum, community college leaders faced the difficult task of establishing the community college
as a unique institution in the minds of students and policy makers, among
others.

Today, community college leaders have more than a century of history
to build on, and although a politics of purpose continues, the purpose of
the contemporary community college has largely been consolidated into a
comprehensive mission: "There may be some misunderstanding over the
community services function, especially in noncredit offerings, and what
it means to provide open access, but the mission is generally understood"
(Vaughan, 1997, p. 36). Nonetheless, community college leaders must not
become complacent. The American Association of Community Colleges
(AACC, 2013) recommends that leaders "always have a succinct pocket
speech that is consistent with the mission, vision, and priorities of the institution" (p. 9). Communicating the unique purposes of the community
college remains an important public relations task.

Mission Statements as Management Strategy

As indicated by this discussion, a close reading of the early literature on
the community college (particularly the *Junior College Journal*)[1] shows that
early community college leaders did not use the term "mission" in reference
to institutional purposes. Instead, institutional goals were discussed broadly
as the community college movement, the community college philosophy, or
simply the purpose of the community college.

In 1973, the American Association of Community and Junior Colleges
(AACJC) board of directors crafted a mission for the association. The statement "grew out of a careful look at how community colleges were developing and how they should continue to develop in view of the evident needs

in our society" (Yarrington, 1975, p. 9). The AACJC mission statement prompted individual colleges to consider their own missions. As one example, Elinor Multer (1970/1971) described a master plan at Brookdale Community College. A vital component of this plan was to consolidate the college's purposes and philosophies into a concise mission statement. Within a decade, missioning had become widespread within higher education contexts (Keller, 1983).

Despite the ubiquity of mission statements, their effectiveness as a management strategy is not well understood. Two relevant studies represent a step in the right direction, however. In a content-oriented analysis of 172 community college mission statements, Abelman and D'Alessandro (2008) examined the organizing functions of the mission statement. Analytical categories in this study included the extent to which mission statements (a) represented a clear, compelling, and shared mission; (b) clarified organizational complexity; (c) addressed relative advantage; and (d) described observable goals. Abelman (2011) used a similar framework when analyzing mission statements of tribal colleges. This work established categories for examining mission statements, but the extent to which missioning contributes to institutional outcomes remains largely unexplored.

Within the broader management literature, missioning may be associated with higher levels of organizational performance, but these relations are nuanced and likely mediated by strategic, structural, and tactical variables (Baetz & Bart, 1998; Bart & Baetz, 1998; Covin, Slevin, & Schultz, 1994). In terms of function, Swales and Rogers (1995) observed that corporate mission statements were designed to promote "buy-in" among employees. Stallworth Williams (2008) showed how mission statements may create both an internal and external ethos and sense of identity among higher performing Fortune 1000 companies.

Mission Statement as Sensemaking

The mission statement "is the fountain from which all else flows" (Vaughan, 1997, p. 47). Missioning is central to organizational strategizing for community college leaders. As the AACC (2013) recognizes, however, a college's mission is not simply a product of internal decision making; rather, it is the product of an interaction among the college and its institutional environment: "An effective community college leader promotes the success of all students, strategically improves the quality of the institution, and sustains the community college mission based on *knowledge of the organization, its environment, and future trends*" (p. 6, emphasis added). This leadership competency explicitly recognizes the interaction of the college and its institutional environment. This environment is increasingly chaotic, however. As a result, community college leaders struggle not only to apprehend cultural, political, and economic trends but also to define the implications for

New Directions for Community Colleges • DOI: 10.1002/cc

local campuses. The mission statement, then, can be thought of as a textual manifestation of sensemaking.

According to Weick (2009), "sensemaking starts with chaos" (p. 133). Within chaotic environments, sensemaking occurs as organizational members "attempt to order the intrinsic flux of human action, to channel it toward certain ends, to give it a particular shape, through generalizing and institutionalizing particular meanings and rules" (cited in Tsoukas & Chia, 2002, p. 570). Sensemaking poses challenges for organizational leaders, however. Communities, their colleges, and the educators therein will inevitably vary in the ways they make sense of the college's environment (Ayers, 2005b); "multiple theories develop about what is happening and what needs to be done" (Weick, 2009, p. 48). Given the diversity of perceptions and opinions, it is unlikely that organizational members will cohere around any given statement of mission. Connell and Galasinski (1998) agree:

> it seems improbable that the achievement of institutional consensus, which is one of the purposes of producing and publishing [statements of] missions, can be realized, not just because the context is one in which there has been explicit debate about fundamental purposes, but also precisely because they fashion axiomatic knowledge. (p. 462)

Connell and Galasinski conclude that the academic mission statement is an act of negotiation. For community colleges, missioning involves an internal contest for resources, "including competition for funds, competition for attention, and competition to serve as the embodiment of the 'real mission' of the community college" (Vaughan, 1997, p. 39).

If the academic mission statement is an act of negotiation, it presents an acute challenge for leaders of an institution known as the contradictory college (Dougherty, 1994). Nonetheless, organizational leaders must make sense of the college's environment and distill this knowledge into a concise mission statement:

> For an organization to act, its knowledge must undergo two transformations: (1) it has to be textualized so that it becomes a unique representation of the otherwise multiply distributed understandings; (2) it has to be voiced by someone who speaks on behalf of the network and its knowledge. (Weick, 2009, p. 4)

In other words, absent an understanding of its purpose, a community college may fail to act strategically. To the extent that the community college mission statement functions as sensemaking, a college and its community must constantly reflect on the match between its mission and a turbulent environment.

There is one more point to add regarding the complexity of the institutional environment: it is permeated with ideologies and assumptions.

The decades prior to and following the turn of the century marked a period of neoliberalism (Levin, 2001)—a set of ideologies and assumptions which entered into community college statements of mission (Ayers, 2005a). In an analysis of 421 community college mission statements, Ayers (2010) identified a tension between neoliberal discourses of globalization on the one hand and those associated with global citizenship on the other.

Community college mission statements continue to evolve. Ayers (2015) compared mission statements from 2004 and those from the 2012–2013 academic year. The analysis suggested that mission statements have evolved along four trajectories. More recent mission statements were statistically more likely to include discourses appertaining to credentialing structures, pedagogies, practices, and curriculum goals. More important, perhaps, Ayers (2015) observed an emerging strategic discourse of sustainability. The more recent mission statements forewarned that a comprehensive mission may not be sustainable, given limited resources.

If resources continue to wane, community colleges may commit to a narrower mission. Indeed, the effectiveness of the community college financial model has come into question, as have accretion models of mission expansion. Quite possibly, emerging strategic discourses of sustainability indicate a point of crisis in which lack of resources mitigates against the comprehensive community college mission. If so, institutional changes register textually as community college leaders use the mission statement as a public relations document, a management strategy, and an act of sensemaking.

Note

1. The flagship publication of the American Association of Community Colleges was originally titled *Junior College Journal* (1930) and assumed different titles over the years: *Community and Junior College Journal* (1972), *Community Technical and Community College Journal* (1985), and finally *Community College Journal* (1992).

References

Abelman, R. (2011). The Institutional Vision of Tribal Community Colleges. *Community College Journal of Research and Practice, 35*(7), 513–538.

Abelman, R., & Dalessandro, A. (2008). The institutional vision of community colleges: Assessing style as well as substance. *Community College Review, 35*, 306–335.

American Association of Community Colleges. (2013). *AACC competencies for community college leaders* (2nd ed.). Washington, DC: Author. Retrieved from http://www.aacc.nche.edu/newsevents/Events/leadershipsuite/Documents/AACC_Core_Competencies_web.pdf

American Association of Junior Colleges. (1952). Junior college world. *Junior College Journal, 22*(9).

Apple, C. (2015). *World War II mission symbols.* Retrieved from http://history.blogs.delaware.gov/2015/09/03/world-war-ii-mission-symbols/

Ayers, D. F. (2005a). Neoliberal ideology in community college mission statements: A critical discourse analysis. *Review of Higher Education, 28*, 527–549.

Ayers, D. F. (2005b). Organizational climate in its semiotic aspect: A postmodern community college undergoes renewal. *Community College Review, 33*(1), 1–21.

Ayers, D. F. (2010). Community colleges and the politics of sociospatial scale. *Higher Education, 62*, 303–314.

Ayers, D. F. (2015). Credentialing structures, pedagogies, practices, and curriculum goals: Trajectories of change in community college mission statements. *Community College Review, 43*, 191–214.

Baetz, M. C., & Bart, C. K. (1998). A comparison of mission statements and their rationales in innovative and non-innovative firms. *International Journal of Technology Management, 16*(1), 64–67.

Bart, C. K., & Baetz, M. C. (1998). The relationship between mission statements and firm performance: An exploratory study. *Journal of Management Studies, 35*(6), 823–853.

Birnbaum, R. (2001). *Management fads in higher education: Where they come from, what they do, why they fail.* San Francisco: Jossey-Bass.

Campbell, D. S. (1930). *A critical study of the stated purposes of the junior college.* Nashville, TN: George Peabody College for Teachers.

Chadwick, R. D. (1947). Cooperation pays dividends. *Junior College Journal, 16*(7), 305–307.

Connell, I., & Galasinski, D. (1998). Academic mission statements: An exercise in negotiation. *Discourse & Society, 9*, 457–479.

Covin, J. G., Slevin, D. P., & Schultz, R. L. (1994). Implementing strategic missions: Effective strategic, structural and tactical choices. *Journal of Management Studies, 31*(4), 481–505.

Dougherty, K. J. (1994). *The contradictory college: The conflicting origins, impacts, and futures of the community college.* Albany: State University of New York Press.

Drucker, P. (1973). *Management: Tasks, responsibilities, practices.* New York: Harper & Row.

Fairclough, N. (2015). *Language and power* (3rd ed.). London: Routledge.

Keller, G. (1983). *Academic strategy: The management revolution in American higher education.* Baltimore, MD: Johns Hopkins University Press.

Kuhns, E. (1974). Organizing for change. *Community and Junior College Journal, 44*(5), 16–17.

Levin, J. S. (2001). *Globalizing the community college: Strategies for change in the twenty-first century.* New York: Palgrave.

McCoy, J. H. (1947). Editorial. *Junior College Journal, 17*(7), 1.

Multer, E. (1970/1971). Master planning: A source of dividends. *Junior College Journal, 41*(4), 18–21.

Orwig, B., & Finney, R. Z. (2007). Analysis of the mission statements of AACSB-accredited schools. *Competitiveness Review, 17*(4), 261–273.

Southern Association of Colleges and Schools. (2012). *The principles of accreditation: Foundation for quality enhancement.* Decatur, GA: Author. Retrieved from http://www.sacscoc.org/pdf/2012PrinciplesOfAcreditation.pdf

Stallworth Williams, L. (2008). The mission statement: A corporate reporting tool with a past, present, and future. *Journal of Business Communication, 45*(2), 94–119. https://doi.org/10.1177/0021943607313989

Stoddard, G. D. (1946). *Report of the United States Educational Mission to Japan.* (Department of State Publication 2579). Washington, DC: U.S. Government Printing Office.

Swales, J. M., & Rogers, P. S. (1995). Discourse and the projection of corporate culture: The mission statement. *Discourse & Society, 6*(2), 223–242.

Tsoukas, H., & Chia, R. (2002). Organizational becoming: Rethinking organizational change. *Organization Science*, *13*(5), 567–582.

Vaughan, G. B. (1997). The community college's mission and milieu: Institutionalizing community-based programming. In E. J. Boone (Ed.), *Community leadership through community-based programming: The role of the community college* (pp. 21–58). Washington, DC: Community College Press.

Weick, K. E. (2009). *Making sense of the organization* (Vol. 2). West Sussex, UK: John Wiley & Sons.

Yarrington, R. (1975). Assessing the community base. *Community and Junior College Journal*, *46*(3), 9–11.

DAVID F. AYERS *is associate professor at Old Dominion University. His research addresses the cultural, political, and economic contexts of the community college mission.*

NEW DIRECTIONS FOR COMMUNITY COLLEGES • DOI: 10.1002/cc

2

This chapter describes the community college challenge to support all learners to succeed in college and enter the middle class as citizens, parents, and workers.

Social Justice and the Community College Mission

Cynthia M. Heelan, Gail O. Mellow

For 106 years, beginning with the founding of Joliet Community College in Illinois, the community college has had an implicit social contract with America to prepare citizens and workers (now 45% of all learners) for entry into the middle class. That contract with America began as a disruptive force, seeking to educate the "top 100%" of students, as former Under Secretary of Education Martha Kanter stated (personal communication, 2008). As the percentage of Americans who see themselves as middle class declines (from 61% in 2000 to 51% in 2015), the focus of social justice becomes even more imperative for this contract (Newport, 2016). This deeply democratic impulse animates community colleges and drives their mission. The contract with America has evolved to be broad, as community colleges now form the major pathway for skills development in an economy that requires midlevel skills to survive. The various pathways provided by community colleges serve as a ladder for maintaining equity in our communities. Through supporting transfer to baccalaureate-granting institutions, low-income learners as well as adult students find a first step into or a reentry into the middle class.

A different light was thrown on the role of higher education after the 2016 presidential election. Not only is there a need to understand the social justice implications of not getting a college degree for youth, but there is a growing resentment among older, predominantly White Americans, as they are pushed out of an economy that previously provided family-sustaining wages to people with only a high school education (Johnson, 2016). The economy is unforgiving to those it leaves behind for lack of education. Community colleges' role in creating a just and equitable society is as compelling for this group of adults and potentially provides a unique opportunity for rethinking the role of education and training for displaced workers in a global

NEW DIRECTIONS FOR COMMUNITY COLLEGES, no. 180, Winter 2017 © 2017 Wiley Periodicals, Inc.
Published online in Wiley Online Library (wileyonlinelibrary.com) • DOI: 10.1002/cc.20277

economy. Alone among postsecondary educational sectors, community colleges offer easy access to lifelong learning opportunities for retooling, career changes, and advancement.

Leadership That Makes It Happen

Rost (1991) offers a definition for leadership that can be a guide to community college leaders as they seek to maintain this contract for social justice with America. He sees leadership as "an influence relationship among leaders and followers who intend real changes that reflect their mutual purposes" (p. 102). He believes the dynamic interaction between leaders and followers has been greatly overlooked. Rost also encourages greater collaboration among educators, practitioners, and scholars. He argues the transition from an industrial paradigm (top down) to a postindustrial paradigm (collaborative and consensual) of leadership is crucial to serving societal needs. Faculty members, support staff, students, and the leadership cabinet are a wealth of ideas and insight. They are all important in clarifying and implementing the many strategies identified that ensure student success.

Although seeking input can be challenging when there is conflict and disagreement, consensus, as described by Cleveland (2002), is the "acquiescence of those who care supported by the apathy of those who don't" (p. 162). This approach to consensus allows all parties to consider the common good and to "acquiesce" when it is needed in order to move an idea forward.

Dovetailing Cleveland's idea of consensus with Rost's idea of mutual influence among those who intend deep change that reflects mutual purpose (common good) describes the kind of leadership needed in community colleges today. Given the context in which community colleges exist today, leaders must be bold in order to fulfill our contract with America.

Supporting Students

The diverse demographics of the United States can be sliced into many categories—race, income, ethnicity, immigration status. No matter how you slice it, community colleges' focus on serving all of these disenfranchised groups eclipses all other sectors of higher education (Carnevale & Strohl, 2010). This means community colleges serve those who are the most in need of support in order to succeed in college.

Multiple measures provide evidence of the kinds of support community college students require. Low levels of academic competence among recent high school graduates require community colleges, as open access institutions, to focus attention on supporting skill development to provide foundational mathematics, reading, writing, and English comprehension in order for students to succeed in college. More than 70% of high school seniors are in need of assistance in reading, math, and writing when they arrive at college, any college, and 42% of them enroll in a community college as first-time freshmen (U.S. Department of Education, 2014). Persons of color and low-income people continue to struggle to realize the American dream. Being born poor or non-White can often prove a difficult hurdle in the U.S. educational system. However, by 2030 the United States will no longer have a White majority, so there is particular urgency in the social contract of community colleges to serve the current 37.9% of persons living in the United States (U.S. Census, 2014) and the 46% of community college students who represent a racial or ethnic group other than White (American Association of Community Colleges, 2016). Leadership in community colleges must be bold in fostering the programs that can truly make a difference in student learning for all students.

Serving such diverse student needs not only poses a challenge for leadership to understand the policy implications of curricular design and measurement of curricular effectiveness but also adds to the advocacy community college leaders must advance to obtain the funding necessary for these programs.

Programs That Support the Community College Demographic

Programs required to support the students enrolled in community colleges have been researched extensively. One example is federal TRIO programs that increase success rates among students who are from low-income, first-generation families or who have a disability. Many community colleges are now designing success programs for ALL learners, and there is much to learn from the TRIO programs that experienced success with the most challenged learners for 50 years. The 3-year persistence rate at 2-year colleges in 2014 for students enrolled in Student Support Services Program (SSS) was 85.4% (U.S. Department of Education, 2013–2014). These successful TRIO services have the potential to be replicated across the college.

SSS programs assist students in applying for admission to and obtaining financial assistance for transfer to graduate and professional programs. One example of a creative program is LaGuardia Community College's Pushy Moms program. It paired volunteers with experience navigating college applications with low-income, new-immigrant, and first-in-family students to advise them as they went through the process of applying to 4-year colleges and universities. The program served about two dozen high-achieving students in its first round and was successful. Innovation in program designs is essential for results that enable students to successfully begin their college careers, persist in their studies, and, ultimately, earn bachelor's degrees ("Pushy Moms," 2016).

Many of the best programs with documented results cost upwards of $1,000 per student. For example, the City University of New York's (CUNY) highly touted Accelerated Study in Associate Programs (http://www1.cuny.edu/sites/asap/), open only to full-time community college students, addresses multiple needs of low-income students. The goal is to help students earn their associate degree in 3 years or less and provide a combination of financial, academic, and personal support, such as metro cards and offsetting of textbook costs. The program costs $4,700 per student annually (Fain, 2015). The cost of these services is far beyond the amount of money most community colleges have available to support students.

The weight of community college's contract with America is heavier than ever as states retreat from funding public higher education (Barr & Turner, 2013). Persistent and bold leadership action to increase funding for community colleges and augment services needed by all is crucial in achieving our contract with America.

Teaching Diverse Students

Community colleges can frequently term themselves "teaching colleges." Digging slightly under this nomenclature, however, reveals that community colleges are more often defined by what faculty do not do (few engage in scholarly research) than by a concerted effort to support engaged pedagogy. To fully embrace the evolving contract with America, much greater emphasis much be placed on new approaches to teaching.

Professional development for community college faculty must reflect an academic culture of faculty autonomy and individuality and must have the professional learning embedded in practice as opposed to a single event or conference (Mellow, Woolis, Klages-Bombich, & Restler, 2015). Further, pedagogy must be evidence based, so that faculty collect the formative assessment of student learning to validate that the pedagogical strategies have their intended impact on student learning, or if not, so that faculty can make alterations in strategy in real time, allowing them to customize approaches to be successful with the students they are currently teaching. The evidence must go further—so that data are collected on the professional development activity itself, ensuring that faculty are not only engaged but actively using what they are learning as a result of the professional development. There must be affordances to make the teaching itself visible, so that faculty can engage in a self-reflective practice that deepens their professional understanding of their own actions. Finally, professional development should occur in a supportive environment of peers, so that the scholarly actions can be collectively and collegially reviewed, providing ample opportunity for support and questions. LaGuardia Community College, through its Reflective Learning Institute (https://reflectivelearninginstitute.laguardia.edu), is one example of how technology can support deep learning around improvement of teaching practices.

Teaching must also reflect the diversity of students who attend community colleges. As faculty engage in a reflective, dialogic practice of teaching, the process of teaching becomes more engaged and engaging. To connect with students whose life circumstances can be so radically different from the faculty who are teaching them, effective pedagogy leans toward social construction of knowledge and constructivist teaching approaches. The British scholar of college pedagogy, Diana Laurillard (2012), notes that "college teaching is not rocket science, it is much, much harder" (p. 5). Her analysis of teaching includes the multiple dynamic and interactive factors of the students themselves, the content, and the interaction among pedagogy, peers, and content. Supporting a new generation of faculty as they transverse this complex terrain and develop stronger ability to create critical thinkers who are able to shape a rapidly changing world is one of the most effective ways to advance the American dream of economic mobility and social justice.

Leadership within each community college demands a bold strategy that brings faculty, staff, and board members together in a unified approach to addressing the demographic and learning needs of their community. Every individual needs to be passionately aware and committed to this social justice movement. One individual in a course taught by this teacher said to me, "My generation is not interested in a movement." However, it is incumbent on leaders to ensure that people are hired who DO care about this movement and who work together to make it happen.

Fulfilling the Contract

The role of the community college in paving the way for people to be economically viable, to contribute to society as a whole, and to move away from poverty and inequality continues to be a major emphasis and responsibility. Our ability to keep tuition reasonable, to address the individual needs of learners, and to graduate learners with both citizenship and worker skills so that all citizens may realize their full potential is preeminent. Leadership that guides the way for this work is pivotal.

Boldness outside the walls of each community college calls for institutional and national leaders to be involved in the macroeconomics of their region and the country. Speaking at meetings of local organizations, addressing state legislators, and working with national officials at the American Association of Community Colleges and other national educational organizations are crucial. The Economic Policy Institute proposes that, as a nation, we need to use the tools of macroeconomic policy to pursue the full employment that requires a full enough education (Kroeger, Cooke, & Gould, 2016).

The bottom line is that policies will generate demand for U.S. goods and services and therefore demand for workers who provide them. Policies that will bring down unemployment, policies that will give workers more leverage, and policies that will raise workers' wages are the keys to giving young people a fighting chance as they enter the labor market, seek to gain the skills necessary as received in a good education, and pay their bills. Community college leaders must be involved and engaged in working toward implementing these policies. In addition, securing financial support for community colleges is an increasingly important role for all community college leaders.

Community college leaders can be in front of this effort by promoting, locally and nationally, successful efforts within their own institutions: We already pay the minimum wage, provide earned sick leave and paid family leave, and provide undocumented workers a path to citizenship, and we can end any discriminatory practices that contribute to race and gender inequities. Community college leaders need to be part of this national discussion and to influence external action.

If the United States is to keep its promise as a country of opportunity, a place where the conditions of one's birth do not constrain one's life chances, community colleges are essential to its future. Leadership to achieve and fulfill the community college's contract with America requires bold and thoughtful action. Boldness requires that community college leaders recognize their role in enacting the social justice contract. Not only must community colleges create conditions for success for a diverse student population, but, in order to fulfill their contract with America, they must shape curriculum that can make a difference for local economies and national citizenship.

References

American Association of Community Colleges. (2016, February). *Fast facts*. Retrieved from http://www.aacc.nche.edu/AboutCC/Pages/fastfactsfactsheet.aspx

Barr, A., & Turner, S. E. (2013) Expanding enrollments and contracting state budgets: The effect of the great recession on higher education. *Annals of the American Academy of Political and Social Science, 650*(1), 168–193.

Carnevale, A. P., & Strohl, J. (2010). How increasing college access is increasing inequality, and what to do about it. In R. D. Kahlenberg (Ed.), *Rewarding strivers: Helping low-income students succeed in college* (pp. 71–190). New York, NY: Century Foundation Press.

Cleveland, H. (2002). *Nobody in charge: Essays on the future of leadership*. San Francisco, CA: Jossey-Bass.

Fain, P. (2015, February 26). Living up to the hype. *Inside Higher Ed*. https://www.insidehighered.com/news/2015/02/26/accelerated-associate-degree-track-cuny-pays-and-earns-fans

Johnson, R. W. (2016, November 14). Trump: Some numbers. *London Review of Books*. Retrieved from https://www.lrb.co.uk/2016/11/14/rw-johnson/trump-some-numbers

Kroeger, K. T., Cooke, T., & Gould, E. (2016, April 21). *The class of 2016: The labor market is still far from ideal for young graduates*. Washington, DC: Economic Policy Institute. Retrieved from http://www.epi.org/files/pdf/103124.pdf

Laurillard, D. (2012). *Teaching as design science: Building pedagogical patterns for learning and technology*. New York, NY: Routledge.

Mellow, G. O., Woolis, D. D., Klages-Bombich, M., & Restler, S. (2015). *Taking college teaching seriously: Pedagogy matters! Fostering student success through faculty-centered practice improvement*. Sterling, VA: Stylus Publishing, LLC.

Newport, F. (2016). *Gallup Poll. Fewer Americans identify as middle class in recent years*. Retrieved from http://www.gallup.com/poll/182918/fewer-americans-identify-middle-class-recent-years.aspx

"Pushy moms" help students in need transfer to top colleges [Video File]. (2016, November 23). Retrieved from http://www.cbsnews.com/videos/pushy-moms -help-students-in-need-transfer-to-top-colleges/

Rost, J. C. (1991). *Leadership for the twenty-first century*. New York, NY: Praeger.

U.S. Census. (2014). *Census quick facts*. Retrieved from https://www.census.gov/ quickfacts/table/PST045215/00

U.S. Department of Education. (2013–2014). *Student Support Services Program performance and efficiency measure results for 2013–2014*. Retrieved from https://www2 .ed.gov/programs/triostudsupp/sss-efficiency2013-14.doc

U.S. Department of Education. (2014). *The nation's report card*. Washington, DC: U.S. Department of Education, Institute of Education Sciences, National Center for Education Statistics. Retrieved from https://www.nationsreportcard.gov

Cynthia M. Heelan *is retired president of Colorado Mountain College and coauthor with Gail O. Mellow of* Minding the Dream: The Process and Practice of the American Community College *and author of* Heart at Work: Stories about Speaking from the Heart at Work *and* A Matter of Life and Death.

Gail O. Mellow *is president of LaGuardia Community College, coauthor of* Minding the Dream: The Process and Practice of the American Community College, *and coauthor of* Taking College Teaching Seriously, Pedagogy Matters!: Fostering Student Success Through Faculty-Centered Practice Improvement.

3

An important aspect of the community college mission is to educate working adults including those without a high school diploma or its equivalent. Three important changes are forcing community colleges to reevaluate how these services and activities are delivered as well as policies that govern this critical work. These shifts provide a new opportunity for community college leaders to reenvision how they engage local employers, working adults, and underprepared college students.

National Shifts in Adult Basic Education: Workforce Innovation and Opportunity Act, Ability to Benefit, and High School Equivalency Tests

J. Cody Davidson

An important aspect of the community college mission is to educate working adults including those without a high school diploma or its equivalent. This is often accomplished through state-sponsored GED programming. Recently, three nationwide changes have fundamentally changed adult basic and developmental education in U.S. community colleges. First is the Workforce Innovation and Opportunity Act (WIOA), which was signed by President Barak Obama on July 22, 2014, and final regulations were released on June 30, 2016. Second, the partial restoration of the federal Ability to Benefit rule has provided access for concurrently equipping high school dropouts with a high school equivalency diploma and postsecondary credential. Third, GED® Testing Service (GEDTS) has released the fifth edition of the 70-year-old GED® test, and two new high school equivalency tests have entered the market for the first time. The purpose of this article is to present the historical context for these nationwide shifts and describe the current adult basic and developmental education conversation in the context of "the need for workers trained to operate the nation's expanding industries" and "the drive for social equality and greater access to higher education", social forces that Cohen, Brawer, and Kisker noted as giving way to the community college (2014, p. 1).

NEW DIRECTIONS FOR COMMUNITY COLLEGES, no. 180, Winter 2017 © 2017 Wiley Periodicals, Inc.
Published online in Wiley Online Library (wileyonlinelibrary.com) • DOI: 10.1002/cc.20278

Adult Education Act

It is important to have a cursory overview of how federal legislation has supported basic skills acquisition and efforts to provide employment opportunity for low-skilled adults. These long-standing legislative efforts have provided the foundation for the U.S. workforce and are centric to understanding the current Workforce Innnovation and Opportunity Act (WIOA).

Legislative History. The education level of working adults (typically defined as individuals ages 18–64) has always been a concern for citizens and policy makers. As far as 1777, the federal government made funds available for basic skills instruction (i.e., Continental Army). Since that time, other federal laws have been passed involving the education of adults: Morrill Act of 1862, Smith-Lever Act of 1914, Smith-Hughes Act of 1917, Federal Emergency Relief Act of 1933, Library Service Act, and the Government Employees Training Act. The legislation that was most pointedly directed toward increasing the educational level of adults, which was part of President Lyndon Johnson's War on Poverty, was the Adult Basic Education Program established in Title II, part B of the Economic Opportunity Act (EOA) on August 20, 1964 (Public Law [P.L.] No. 88–452). This legislation focused on literacy skills and employment (Eyre, 1998; Tyler, 2005).

Originally, the act was authorized through the Office of Economic Opportunity but administered by the U.S. Office of Education. Initially, the act was to reach persons 18 years of age or older who had completed no more than five grades of school. The 1966 Title III of the amendment to the Elementary and Secondary Act (ESEA; P.L. 89-75) formally transferred the program to the U.S. Office of Education and established the National Advisory Council on Adult Education. In the 1970s (P.L. 91–230, 92–318, 93–380, and 95–561), the authors of the act revised the purpose to focus on adults age 16 and older without a high school diploma, authorized 5% administrative cost (P.L. 91–230), and provided bilingual adult education and teacher training (P.L. 93–380). In the 1980s (P.L. 97-35, 99–500, and 100–297), literacy became a primary concern through the creation of workforce literacy grants and the English literacy grant program (P.L. 100–297), and support for English as a second language was first provided (P.L. 97-35). In the 1990s (P.L. 102–73, 105–220), there was the National Literacy Act of 1991, which was incorporated into the Adult Education Act and the Workforce Investment Act (WIA; 1998) (Adult Education and Family Literacy Act [Title II]), which repealed and replaced the Adult Education Act. The National Literacy Act of 1991 established a National Institute for Literary, included incarcerated individuals, and created indicators for program quality (P.L. 102–73). After WIA, the act was not reauthorized until 2014, when it was titled the Workforce Innovation and Opportunity Act (Eyre, 1998; U.S. Department of Education, 2013).

Workforce Innovation and Opportunity Act. In WIOA, performance and accountability were shared among the four titles that constitute the legislation, which are identified as "core partners": Title I–Workforce Development, Title II–Adult Education and Family Literacy, Title III–Wagner-Peyser Act of 1933, and Title IV–Rehabilitation Act of 1973. In total, WIOA recognizes 19 required partners, which constitute the one-stop delivery system. The one-stop delivery system in each local workforce developmental area is centered around its (one or more) Comprehensive American Job Center, which, in some places, is physically located on the community college campus.

For Title II, WIOA retained the programs, activities, and services of adult education, literacy, workplace adult education and literacy activities, and family literacy activities and added English language acquisition activities, integrated English literacy and civics education (now codified), workforce preparation activities, and integrated education and training.

Performance and Accountability.   There are six common "primary indicators of performance" for which all four titles are commonly accountable. Each partner is solely accountable for its performance on each indicator as well as each partner is commonly accountable for the combined performance for each indicator. The primary indicators of performance include employment in the second and fourth quarters after exit, median earnings, credential attainment, measurable skill gains, and effectiveness in serving employers. For the credential attainment measure, the core programs will be accountable for participants who are attempting to obtain a high school equivalency diploma and those enrolled in postsecondary programs including eligible training providers programs, which, in many states, are predominantly provided through the community and technical colleges. Likewise, the effectiveness in serving employers measure may include the community and technical college departments (e.g., workforce solutions) that directly serve local business and industry.

Integrated Education and Training Models.   Similar to state legislation aligning K–12 and postsecondary-level career/technical education (Zinth, 2015a), the WIOA legislation focuses on career pathways. The core partners are charged with leveraging one-stop delivery system services while creating career pathways for all participants (National Career Pathways Network, 2016). As part of the career pathway, Title II legislation focuses on integrated education and training (IET) models, which combine the adult education and literacy activities with workforce preparation activities and training. Thus, students are able to quickly gain the necessary education and training, concurrently and contextually, to fill current and future local job market needs (Carnevale, Smith, & Strohl, 2013). Prior to WIOA, a number of transition to postsecondary education models for adult education students had been proposed and examined (Alamprese, 2005; Garvey & Grobe, 2011; Rutschow & Crary-Ross, 2014; Zafft, Kallenbach, & Spohn, 2006); however, WIOA's emphasis is not on sequential transitioning from adult basic to postsecondary education but concurrent enrollment in both. The IET model is clearly exemplified in Jobs for the Future's Accelerating Opportunity initiative and Washington state's Integrated Basic Education and Skills Training (I-BEST) model (Wachen, Jenkins, Belfield, & Van Noy, 2012; Wachen, Jenkins, & Van Noy, 2011; Zeidenberg, Cho, & Jenkins, 2010). This is particularly important for individuals without a high school diploma or equivalency because this group also lacks other types of alternative credentials such as licenses, or professional of educational certificates that are more prevalent with increased levels of formal education (Ewert & Kominski, 2014).

To create these models, adult education programs should form strategic partnerships with Title I eligible training providers, such as community and technical colleges. Community college leadership plays a pivotal role in this relationship because many community colleges are Title II service providers and Title I eligible training providers.

Ability to Benefit.   The Ability to Benefit provision (Higher Education Act [HEA]; P.L. 113–235) allows individuals without a high school diploma or its equivalent to be eligible for a federal Pell Grant while attending college courses and adult basic education classes in effort to earn high school equivalency. The Ability to Benefit provision ceased in the Consolidated Appropriations Act of 2012 (Davidson, 2014) then was partially restored through the passing of the Consolidated and Further Continuing Act of 2015 (P.L. 114–235). One year later, the Consolidations Appropriation Act of 2016 (P.L. 114–113) redefined career pathway to fully align with the definition in WIOA. To be eligible for federal Pell Grants, students must be enrolled in a career pathway and the adult education instruction must be "articulated and contextualized" within the technical training.

GED® Test

Even though the number of students dropping out of high school has declined on the past 4 decades (Stark & Noel, 2015), current population reports show there is still a need for high school equivalency certifications, particularly for foreign-born persons, Hispanics, and adults with disabilities (Ryan & Bauman, 2016). The GED® test has played an important role in the history of the U.S. educational landscape and has practically been the sole means for high school dropouts to earn their high school equivalency for more than 70 years. There has been an extensive amount of research related to the GED® test; studies have examined the GED® earners and noneconomic outcomes (e.g., life satisfaction, health, etc.) and recidivism rates, but primarily in postsecondary, and economic and labor market outcomes. At the same time as the signing of WIOA, new high school equivalency tests were introduced and GEDTS released a fifth GED® test edition.

GED® Test History.   The GED® test is administered by GED® Testing Service, which is an arm of the American Council on Education (ACE). The Commission on Educational Credit and Credentials of the ACE sets the minimum passing scores on the exams.

NEW DIRECTIONS FOR COMMUNITY COLLEGES • DOI: 10.1002/cc

The GED® test was formed in 1942 to certify World War II veterans without a high school diploma who had the ability to benefit in postsecondary education, thus making the returnees eligible for G.I. Bill benefits. The first test was administered in 1943, and in 1947, New York became the first state to administer the test to high school dropouts (Tyler, 2003). For the first time, more civilians took the GED® test than military personnel in the 1960s (Boesel, Alsalam, & Smith, 1998). The second GED® test edition was released in 1978 and the third in 1988. "Until 1997 . . . many states chose higher standards than those the ACE set, generating substantial variation across states in the standards required to pass the GED® exams. In 1997, the ACE raised the required minimum, and since that time, most states have had the same GED® passing standard" (Tyler, 2005, p. 47). The fourth GED® test edition was released in 2002.

Changes to the fifth edition of the GED® test included cost (i.e., from $60 to $120), administration, and content (Clymer, 2012; Shaffer, 2015). Previously, students attempting to earn their high school equivalency diploma had access to the GED® test at testing centers and at places such as high schools, community colleges, prisons, churches, etc.; however, the nonprofit American Council on Education formed a public–private partnership with Pearson VUE testing centers to deliver the GED® test, so starting with the fifth edition, the GED® test is now a computer-based test administered only at Pearson VUE approved testing facilities. The test content is now in alignment with college and career readiness standards, which has drawn varied comments from policy centers (Clymer, 2012; Halbert, 2016; Pham, Waterous, & Jones, 2015; Reinhard & Harris, 2013) and sharp criticism from media outlets (Levin, 2015; McGraw, 2014). Shaffer's (2015) survey of GED®-only state administrators noted that adult education instructors were more vocal regarding the difficulty of the new GED® test than were GED®-seeking students.

Two new high school equivalency tests have been introduced into the market: the Educational Testing Service's (ETS) High School Equivalency Test (HiSET) and the Data Recognition Corporation/CTB's Test Assessing Secondary Completion (TASC). The three tests vary based on length, item type, formats available, and cost (Zinth, 2015b). Even though the new GED® test edition has been criticized because of the low number of test takers and a lower passing rate, the same (i.e., fewer test takers and a lower passing rate) has been reported in Indiana, which no longer uses the GED® test but adopted the TASC (Slagter, 2015).

In January, 2016, 2 years after the release of the latest test edition, GED® Testing Service announced a "recalibrated" passing score from 150 to 145. Additionally, students passing the GED® test with a score of 165 or higher would be considered "college ready" and students scoring 175 or higher would also be recommended for college credit in that subject area (i.e., three credit hours in math, social studies, and science and an additional credit in language arts). This decision was based on 18 months of test taker data, conversations with state policy makers and elected officials, and external validation with experts (Fain, 2016; Mortrude, 2016). The three-tier passing score range allows for the development of career pathways for GED® earners because now there is a direct connection between GED® test scores and college placement. For community colleges that adopt 165 or higher as an official indicator of college readiness, these GED® earners will be able to enroll directly into college-level, credit-bearing courses rather than return adult basic or developmental education courses. Thus, adult educators may now work with their college-bound students toward achieving this score.

Alternative Pathways to High School Equivalency. Even though exam-certified (e.g., GED® test) high school equivalency students have been criticized as not being equivalent to high school graduates (Cameron & Heckman, 1993), exam certification is not the only means to a state-certified high school equivalency diploma.

One way is the National External Diploma Program (NEDP), which is a competency-based program without formal classes. Students demonstrate mastery in 70 competencies across 10 content areas and an individual competency. The program is administered by the Comprehensive Adult Student Assessment System (CASAS) and has at least one site in California, Connecticut, Indiana, Maryland, New York, Rhode Island, Virginia, and Washington, DC. Historical data show the NEDP alternative is often accessed by adults over the age of 25 (average age is 31), females, African Americans, and employed persons. Hawaii and Vermont and other states' local educational entities have developed their own competency-based programs (Clymer, 2012).

Also, some states provide a high school equivalency diploma to students who earn postsecondary credit. For example, Wisconsin, which has multiple pathways for adults to earn a high school equivalency diploma, will award a high school equivalency diploma based on a student earning 24 semester credits or 32 quarter credits (in all areas of state graduation requirements) and passing a civics test. In Pennsylvania, students may earn a Commonwealth Secondary School Diploma by earning 30 college credits from a U.S.-accredited institution of postsecondary education. A third example is the state of New York, which has a high school equivalency diploma option for students who have earned 24 credits at an approved institution.

Conclusion

Since its legislative inception, more than 50 years ago, adult basic and developmental education has clearly aligned with the mission of the community college to develop a trained workforce, create social equality, and provide access to higher education. Its latest iteration, WIOA, builds on this rich tradition and even expands the scope of these services. Title II services have a distinct niche within career pathways for adults with low basic skills and high school dropouts, particularly through the partial restoration of the Ability to Benefit and alternative pathways to a high school equivalency. Likewise, pairing these educational services with workforce training raises the value and exposure of adult basic and developmental education. The common measures further demonstrate the importance and accountability Title II programs have within the full scope of the one-stop delivery system. Community and technical colleges have a unique opportunity to facilitate the local implementation and ongoing success of WIOA in their own communities. As a critical community partner and, often, fiscal agent and service deliverer of Title I and II programs, community colleges can be the hub of communication and change that further the creation and sustaining efforts of a trained workforce, social equality, and access to higher education through adult basic and developmental education.

References

Alamprese, J. (2005). *Helping adult learners make the transition to postsecondary education*. Cambridge, MA: Abt Associates.

Boesel, D., Alsalam, N., & Smith, T. M. (1998). Educational and labor market outcomes of GED certification. Washington, DC: National Library of Education, Office of Educational Research and Improvement, U.S. Department of Education.

Cameron, S. V., & Heckman, J. J. (1993). The nonequivalence of high school equivalencies. *Journal of Labor Economics, 11*(1), 1–47.

Carnevale, A. P., Smith, N., & Strohl, J. (2013, June). *Recovery: Job growth and education requirements through 2020*. Washington, DC: Georgetown University, Center on Education and Workforce. Retrieved from https://cew.georgetown.edu/wp-content/uploads/2014/11/Recovery2020.FR_.Web_.pdf

Clymer, C. (2012). *Preparing for the new GED test: What to consider before 2014*. Retrieved from http://www.workingpoorfamilies.org/reports_and_pubs/

Cohen, A. M., Brawer, F. B., & Kisker, C. B. (2014). *The American community college* (6th ed.). San Francisco, CA: Jossey-Bass.

Davidson, J. C. (2014). Changes to Federal Pell Grant eligibility: The effect of policy and program changes on college students at public institutions in Kentucky. *Journal of Student Financial Aid, 43*(3), 111–131.

Ewert, S., & Kominski, R. (2014, January). *Measuring alternative educational credentials: 2012* (Household Economic Studies P70-138). Washington, DC: U. S. Department of Commerce, Economics and Statistics Administration, Census Bureau. Retrieved from https://www.census.gov/prod/2014pubs/p70-138.pdf

Eyre, G. (1998). *History of the Adult Education Act*. National Adult Education Professional Development Consortium. Retrieved from http://www.naepdc.org/issues/AEAHistort.htm

Fain, P. (2016, January 26). New passing score for the GED. *Inside Higher Ed*. Retrieved from https://www.insidehighered.com/quicktakes/2016/01/26/new-passing-score-ged

Garvey, J., & Grobe, T. (2011, May). *From GED to college degree: Creating pathways to postsecondary success for high school dropouts*. Boston, MA: Jobs for the Future. Retrieved from http://www.jff.org/sites/default/files/publications/FromGEDto CollegeDegree_042211.pdf

Halbert, H. (2016, February 18). *GED collapse prevents Ohioans from attaining high school diplomas*. Cleveland, OH: Policy Matters Ohio. Retrieved from http://www.policymattersohio.org/ged-feb2016

Levin, S. (2015, June 3). How the new GED is failing students. *East Bay Express*. Retrieved from http://www.eastbayexpress.com/oakland/how-the-new-ged-is-failing-students/Content?oid=4315157

McGraw, D. (2014, December 17). Nearly 500,000 fewer Americans will pass the GED in 2014 after a major overhaul to the test. Why? And who's left behind. *Cleveland Scene*. Retrieved from https://www.clevescene.com/cleveland/after-a-major-overhaul-to-the-ged-test-in-2014-18000-fewer-ohioans-will-pass-the-exam-this-year-than-last-along-with-nearly-500000-across/Content?oid=4442224

Mortrude, J. (2016, January 29). *GED scoring change provides opportunity for career pathway alignment*. Washington, DC: CLASP. Retrieved from http://www.clasp.org/issues/postsecondary/in-focus/ged-change-provides-opportunity-for-career-pathway-alignment

National Career Pathways Network. (2016, April 28). *Dear colleagues letter*. Retrieved from http://www.ncpn.info/2016-downloads/CP-JointLetterFinal-4-22-2016.pdf

Pham, D., Waterous, F., & Jones, R. (2015, December 7). *Expanding opportunity: The need for multiple high school equivalency assessment options in Colorado*. Denver, CO: Bell Policy Center. Retrieved from http://www.bellpolicy.org/research/expanding-opportunity-need-multiple-high-school-equivalency-assessment-options-colorado

Reinhard, C., & Harris, J. (2013, June). *The GED matters: Making sure Maine gets the right equivalency test to meet the needs of low-income adult learners*. Augusta, ME: Maine Center for Economy Policy. Retrieved from the http://www.mecep.org/the-ged-matters/

Rutschow, E. Z., & Crary-Ross, S. (2014, January). *Beyond the GED: Promising models for moving high school dropouts to college*. New York, NY: MDRC. Retrieved from http://www.mdrc.org/sites/default/files/Beyond_the_GED_FR_0.pdf

Ryan, C. L., & Bauman, K. (2016, March). *Educational attainment in the United States: 2015* (Current Population Reports P20-578). Washington, DC: U.S. Department of Commerce, Economics and Statistics Administration, Census Bureau. Retrieved from https://www.census.gov/content/dam/Census/library/publications/2016/demo/p20-578.pdf

Shaffer, B. (2015, May). The Changing Landscape of High School Equivalency in the US: Options, issues, and improvement strategies. Retrieved from the CLASP website: www.clasp.org/sites/default/files/public/resources-and-publications/publication-1/The-Changing-Landscape-of-High-School-Equivalency-in-the-U.S.-Final.pdf

Slagter, L. (2015, April 21). Test participation, pass rates drop with new high school equivalency test. *Kokomo Tribune*. Retrieved from http://www.kokomotribune.com/news/test-participation-pass-rates-drop-with-new-high-school-equivalency/article_81480b58-e796-11e4-8c78-67f117c0a1b8.html

Stark, P., & Noel, A. M. (2015, June). *Trends in high school dropout and completion rates in the United States: 1972–2012* (NCES 2015-015). Washington, DC: U.S. Department of Education, National Center for Education Statistics.

Tyler, J. H. (2003). Economic benefits of the GED: Lessons from research. *Review of Educational Research, 73*(3), 369–405.

Tyler, J. H. (2005). The General Education Diploma (GED) credential: History, current research, and directions for policy and practice. In J. Comings, B. Garner, & C. Smith (Eds.), *Review of adult learning and literacy* (Vol. 5, pp. 45–84). Mahwah, NJ: Erlbaum.

U.S. Department of Education. (2013, November). *An American heritage—federal adult education: A legislative history 1964–2013*. Washington, DC: U.S. Department of Education, Office of Vocational and Adult Education.

Wachen, J., Jenkins, D., Belfield, C., & Van Noy, M. (2012, December). *Contextualized college transition strategies for adult basic skills students: Learning from Washington State's I-BEST program model.* New York, NY: Columbia University, Community College Research Center.

Wachen, J., Jenkins, D., & Van Noy, M. (2011). Integrating basic skills and career-technical instruction: Findings from a field study of Washington State's I_BEST Model. *Community College Review, 39*(2), 136–159.

Zafft, C., Kallenbach, S., & Spohn, J. (2006, December). *Transitioning adults to college: Adult basic education program models.* Cambridge, MA: National Center for the Study of Adult Learning and Literacy. Retrieved from http://www.collegetransition.org/docs/nctntransitionpaper.pdf

Zeidenberg, M., Cho, S.-W., & Jenkins, D. (2010, September). *Washington State's Integrated Basic Education and Skills Training Program (I-BEST): New evidence of effectiveness.* New York, NY: Columbia University, Community College Research Center.

Zinth, J. (2015a, October). *Aligning K–12 and postsecondary career pathways with workforce needs.* Denver, CO: Education Commission of the States. Retrieved from http://www.ecs.org/clearinghouse/01/21/31/12131.pdf

Zinth, J. (2015b, July). *GED, HiSET and TASC test: A comparison of high school equivalency assessments.* Denver, CO: Education Commission of the States. Retrieved from http://www.ecs.org/clearinghouse/01/20/38/12038.pdf

J. Cody Davidson, Ph.D., *a former community and technical college administrator and adjunct instructor, is the executive director of administration and accountability for Kentucky Adult Education at the Council on Postsecondary Education in Frankfort, Kentucky.*

4

This chapter explores the changing nature of how students experience postsecondary education that results in a considerable amount of "swirl" between institutions. Although the traditional notion of "vertical" transfer from a community college to a university continues to be an important aspect of the community college mission, the varying patterns of mobility between institutions will have significant implications for students, the costs they incur, and their ultimate success.

The Evolving Transfer Mission and Student Mobility

Christopher A. Baldwin

Conventional wisdom is that higher education attainment will lead to increased earnings over a person's lifetime. Increased credential attainment will not only improve an individual's prospects for higher income and the ability to support a family, but it will also enhance the collective economic vitality of the state in which he or she lives. Efforts to increase attainment levels are inclusive of all degrees and certificates, but most students aspire to the baccalaureate degree. Reflecting the historical task of community colleges as "junior colleges" to prepare students for the rigors of attending a 4-year university, a 2011 National Center for Education Statistics study found that 80% of community college students intend to get a bachelor's degree (Horn & Skomsvold, 2011). Although this research found that only 17% of these students had actually earned the bachelor's 6 years later, it is clear that a large percentage of community colleges students intend to transfer to a university and get a bachelor's degree. Even if students fall short of meeting this goal, their stated expectation is indicative of why the transfer function continues to be so central to the mission of community colleges.

In a 2012 American Association of Community Colleges (AACC) brief titled *Transfer: An Indispensable Part of the Community College Mission*, the author describes community colleges as playing "a substantial if not always appreciated role in bachelor's degree attainment" (Mullin, 2012, p. 5). A recent report from the National Student Clearinghouse (NSC) quantifies this relationship showing that 46% of 4-year degrees awarded nationally in

NEW DIRECTIONS FOR COMMUNITY COLLEGES, no. 180, Winter 2017 © 2017 Wiley Periodicals, Inc.
Published online in Wiley Online Library (wileyonlinelibrary.com) • DOI: 10.1002/cc.20279

the 2013–2014 academic year went to students with previous enrollment in a 2-year institution (NSC Research Center, 2015).

Given the extent to which students are taking community college courses as part of their goal of earning a 4-year degree, it is critical to ensure transfer pathways are streamlined and clear transfer and articulation policies are in place. However, NSC also helps us understand that the mobility of students between postsecondary institutions is more complex and that the traditional vertical transfer path from a community college to a university represents only a portion of the trajectories students actually take through higher education. Students are increasingly swirling between multiple postsecondary institutions, and as a result, practitioners and researchers need to examine and plan for how other enrollment patterns may affect their students and the college mission.

In general, "traditional" vertical transfer from a community college to a 4-year institution has received the bulk of the attention from policy makers and scholars with the nature and outcomes associated with other patterns of mobility remaining largely unexplored. This chapter highlights these other patterns and, alongside a discussion about traditional vertical transfer, suggests implications for the future transfer mission of the community college.

Toward a More Nuanced View of Student Mobility

In a series of reports, the NSC has used their comprehensive data set on enrollment and completion to analyze the variation of students' mobility patterns. The patterns detailed in these reports have challenged conventional thinking about transfer nationally, while confirming widespread student "swirl" among institutions. The descriptive analyses provided by the NSC suggest that practitioners and policy makers need more sophisticated strategies and policies that recognize the mobility of students and facilitate successful transitions and outcomes.

In their 2015 report *Transfer and Mobility: A National View of Student Movement in Postsecondary Institutions*, NCS highlighted these complex patterns for a cohort of students by examining initial enrollments and transfer rates, the students' destination after their first transfer, and the timing of their initial transfer (Shapiro, Dundar, Wakhungu, Yuan, Harrell, 2015). This analysis found that nearly as many students in the 2008 cohort transferred from 4-year institutions as they did from 2-year institutions. This pattern raises an important question about how the credits of students who transfer are treated at the receiving institutions. Very few state transfer policies or institutional practices were designed for students' transfer *from* a university and there has been very limited study of how these patterns affect student outcomes.

Examining where students end up after their first transfer, the NCS report sheds light on some counterintuitive patterns. With the exception of students who started at a private nonprofit 4-year institution, the most common destination for transfer students in the 2008 cohort was a public 2-year college. Focusing more closely on transitions from public 4-year institutions, 38%, or 160,650, of students who started at these institutions transferred to a public 2-year college. These numbers *do not* include students enrolled in 4-year institution who take courses at the local community college over the summer. Instead, these are students who matriculate to a public 2-year college. This notion of reverse transfer, to which we return later in the chapter, is not a new phenomenon, but research about this pattern is scant and state or institutional policies to support this kind of transition have been largely nonexistent.

Another pattern that is worth exploring from the recent NSC mobility report is the timing of when students first transfer. The highest percentage of students transferring occurred in their second year regardless of where they started. The second highest percentage was in the third year and then the pattern trails off in fourth, fifth, and sixth year. What is striking is that nearly half of all students who transferred (from any sector) did so in the third year or later. It is worth noting that only 12% of the students in any sector were enrolled exclusively part time. In community colleges students, 11.8% were exclusively part time, 29% were exclusively full time, and 54.1% had mixed enrollment. This suggests that given the amount of time students are spending at community colleges, they may be accumulating a substantial number of credits, which increases the stakes for the transferability *and applicability* of those credits toward their program of study. Conversely, students may be stalled in developmental sequences and accumulating very few credits toward transfer. Either scenario complicates seamless transfer to the baccalaureate institution.

The findings of the NSC mobility research demonstrate much more complex patterns of student enrollment and movement between institutions than have been assumed in policy circles and in the research literature related to transfer. The next section of this chapter explores some of these nontraditional patterns of mobility and enrollment. We then return to the traditional notion of vertical transfer from community colleges to universities to highlight new thinking about how institutional leaders and policy makers should be thinking differently about this mainstay of the 2-year college mission.

Patterns of Lateral and Reverse Transfer

Lateral transfer and reverse transfer are "nonlinear" attendance patterns that have received little attention in the research literature. The empirical evidence that does exist indicates that these alternative patterns of transfer are more common than conventional wisdom would suggest (Bahr, 2012; Shapiro et al., 2015), which has implications for how community college practitioners should think about their institutions' transfer mission.

New Directions for Community Colleges • DOI: 10.1002/cc

Starting with lateral transfer, the NSC report (Shapiro et al., 2015) indicates that 37% of students who begin at a public 2-year college transferred to *another* public 2-year college and 36% of those who started in a public 4-year institution transferred to *another* public 4-year institution. Given the rising cost of college and the debt students are accruing, these patterns raise important issues about how the credits students are accumulating are being handled by the receiving institution. For community colleges specifically, which traditionally think more about students transferring out than in, there is limited understanding about the intake processes for students who "transfer in" credits and how they credits are applied to the programs they are pursuing.

Some states have sought to streamline the transferability of a "common core" of courses that often equates to first 30 credits or general education core (Smith, 2010). To the extent that students who transfer laterally are in states with one of these common core agreements and they transfer only general education courses they may not be hurt by a lateral transition. However, a full third of the states do not have this type of agreement, which means institutions set their own requirements that may vary widely. Taken as a whole, this variation increases the likelihood that student transitions will result in lost credits, retaking courses, and, ultimately, greater costs.

Bahr's (2012) research on transfer in California between community colleges provides important insights on student's intentions when moving laterally between institutions. He found that students are balancing college and work schedules and the availability of particular courses in the term when students need them may influence which college they enroll in. A more mobile student population may encounter more barriers to progressing quickly to a degree.

Similar to lateral transfer patterns, there is mounting evidence that a sizable percentage of students are "reverse" transferring from 4-year institutions to community colleges. Again, the NSC report (Shapiro et al., 2015) indicates that among those who transfer from public universities 38% transition "back" to a community college. The patterns are also prevalent in other sectors with 30% and 41% for students transferring from private non-profits and private for-profit schools to community colleges, respectively. The evidence of the frequency of reverse transfer demands more refined thinking by community college practitioners about their approach to institutional policies and practices, which most often assume transitions in the other direction.

Another variant of "reverse transfer" has emerged in the field that is designed to actively encourage student who successfully transferred from a community college to a university to retroactively attain their associate's degree. In 2012, an initiative called *Credit When It's Due* (CWID) was launched with the aim of understanding the process by which transfer students receive an associate degree once they have met the 2-year degree requirements but *after* transferring to a 4-year university. The idea is that students

NEW DIRECTIONS FOR COMMUNITY COLLEGES • DOI: 10.1002/cc

transfer credits from the university to the community college to complete the associate degree requirements, but they do not reenroll in the community college. This is distinct from the approach to reverse transfer in the research literature where students leave the university and actually matriculate at a community college (Taylor, 2015).

Encouragingly this work has led to an increase in dialogue between community colleges and universities about how students experience the transition between their respective institutions. The degrees that have been awarded through this initiative provide yet more evidence that students have different ideas about how they will experience higher education institutions. It also highlights the kinds of barriers existing policies and procedures may create for students to reach their educational goals. Ideally, students would not need to reverse transfer credits to retroactively be awarded the associate degree, but instead, they would understand the value of doing so when they are enrolled in the community college originally. Given the growing preponderance of lateral and reverse transfer students, community colleges need to rethink the traditional transfer mission and adjust to the role of being both a sending *and* a receiving institution if they are going to help their students succeed.

Transfer Students Outcomes

This section examines the historical notion of vertical transfer from a community college to a university. As noted previously, 80% of community college students intend to get a bachelor's degree, but only 17% of these individuals actually achieve this goal after 6 years (Horn & Skomsvold, 2011). The research literature generally indicates that students whose goal is a bachelor's degree will be less likely to attain that credential if they first enroll at a community college (Long & Kurlaender, 2009; Roska & Keith, 2008). Researchers typically attribute the community college "penalty" to problems in academic preparation, student intent, or the lack of student supports at the community college. Research that has controlled for institutional or student characteristics still found that students who started in community colleges were less likely to attain a bachelor's degree than those who began in 4-year institutions (Alfonso, 2006; Long & Kurlaender, 2009).

The open question is why does attendance at community colleges hinder bachelor's degree attainment? Brint and Karabel (1989) argued that the expanding vocational emphasis has diverted capable students to the subbaccalaureate technical programs, but Roska (2006) asserts that the vocational focus itself is not the problem. He observes that the growing emphasis on short-term certificate programs could be diverting students from degree programs. This perspective is logical given that many community college students attend part time, often work multiple jobs, and the pressure to move quickly toward a credential is considerable.

Another perspective on why baccalaureate attainment for those who attend community colleges is lower relates to the students' "social know-how" (Deil-Amen & Rosenbaum, 2003, p. 120). In this study, the authors argue that the knowledge needed to navigate life as a community college student is comparable to that required at a 4-year institution, yet 2-year institutions do not do enough to impart this knowledge to those who enroll. They highlight seven obstacles many community colleges students face because they lack the appropriate knowledge and/or college-going experience via family or friends: (a) bureaucratic hurdles, (b) confusing program choices, (c) student-initiated guidance, (d) limited counselor availability, (e) poor advice from staff, (f) slow detection of costly mistakes, and (g) poor handling of conflicting demands. The recent "guided pathways" work in the community colleges sector is meant to holistically reform the institutions to address these obstacles (Jenkins, Lahr, & Fink, 2017).

The idea of limited social know-how draws on the considerable amount of research about transfer "shock" and the period of adjustment for student who transition from community colleges to universities (Ishitani, 2008). It also suggests that there needs to be a more receptive culture at receiving institutions for transfer students. A literature review on community college transitions and outcomes in 4-year institutions corroborates this notion and suggests to truly understand transfer student success researchers need to incorporate students' experiences in the 4-year institution after transferring to the 4-year institution (Bahr, Toth, Thirolf, & Massé, 2013).

In a 2015 study, Monaghan and Attewell challenged previous research that pointed to lower academic preparation of students transferring from community colleges as the culprit for low bachelor completion rates. They found that completion was primarily influenced by the loss of credits at the university. The study found that fewer than 60% of students were able to transfer most of their credits and as many as 15% of transfer students were not able to transfer any credits at all. In the end, they found the loss of credits after transfer to be the most significant obstacle for students to complete a bachelor's degree. This is further evidenced that the role of the receiving institution in this transition needs to be more closely examined to fully appreciate the outcomes of students.

With the rising cost of higher education, it is likely that a growing number of students will choose to start at more cost-effective community colleges. The proliferation of free community college programs will only accelerate this pattern. Given the already large proportion of community college students whose stated intent is to earn a bachelor's degree, the percentage of students who ultimately transfer from a community college to university will likely increase as well—and intensify the need to improve the efficiency and effectiveness of transfer between institutions.

To begin to address these issues, the Community College Research Center, the College Excellence Program at the Aspen Institute, and the NSC Research Center partnered to provide direction on the way forward. This collaboration focused on articulating a clear set of metrics to understand how institutions and states are performing as it relates to transfer (Jenkins & Fink, 2016). Subsequently, these organizations used the metrics to more closely examine local relationships between community colleges and universities that are proving to be more successful in helping transfer students succeed (Wyner, Deane, Jenkins, & Fink, 2016).

Having a more robust set of transfer metrics is a powerful lever for improvement. Given the variation in transfer outcomes among institutions and across states, this work has illustrated the need to have an approach that addresses both policy and practice. Digging deeper into these differences can shed light on important nuances and help policy makers and practitioners draw lessons from places where students are performing better. Although this collaborative has focused on traditional vertical transfer relationships, there are important lessons that can be drawn for lateral or reverse transfer students as well.

Conclusion—Implications for CCs Moving Forward

The increasing mobility of students coupled with the rising cost of higher education has led many policy makers to look for ways to streamline transitions between institutions and minimize the number of credit hours/courses not accepted or those that need to be repeated. A recent report on increased student mobility among higher education institutions found that states are moving away from "fragmented transfer policies set by individual institutions" to a more coherent approach to transfer and articulation between and among colleges and universities (Millard, 2014, p. 37). Although state adoption and implementation of these policies have varied in the details, the overarching theme is that states are becoming much more prescriptive about how credits should be transferred and accepted at receiving colleges and universities.

The policy developments with transfer and articulation are closely related to the intensifying national movement toward guided programmatic pathways occurring at an increasing number of community colleges (Jenkins, Lahr, & Fink, 2017). As institutions seek to streamline program pathways, colleges are focusing on the full student experience from the time they make their first connection with the college to when they complete a credential and move on to a job or further their education. It is the pathways within colleges and how they intersect with transitions to other institutions that are crucial to consider with transfer policy.

Given the growing preponderance of "nontraditional" transfer patterns described here, the idea of transparent program paths *and* robust student supports is critical for all higher education institutions to embrace. However, to be effective, these reforms must take the varying mobility patterns of students into consideration and not assume students will follow a linear path. The following recommendations are drawn from recent reports from the College Excellence Program at the Aspen Institute and Education Northwest of items states and institutions should consider to streamline student transitions and improve credit mobility (Hodara, Martinez-Wenzl, Stevens, & Mazzeo, 2016; Wyner et al., 2016):

- Make transfer student success a priority and ensure that policies and practices address both the transferability *and* the applicability of credits to a student's program of study.
- Establish clear programmatic pathways that are aligned with labor market demands for all students but pointedly address the needs of undecided students.
- Provide tailored transfer student advising that develops a student's knowledge of the transfer process early in their academic career and establishes milestones to ensure they are on track.
- Improve data systems and conduct research on credit mobility at both the state and institutional levels to determine the effectiveness of policies and practices.

Community colleges have prided themselves on meeting students where they are and helping them move toward their educational goal. The transfer mission has long been a central function of these open-access institutions. Moving forward, colleges need to embrace the mobile student and get better organized as both a sending *and* a receiving institution if they are going to help them succeed.

References

Alfonso, M. (2006). The impact of community college attendance on baccalaureate attainment. *Research in Higher Education, 47,* 873–903.

Bahr, P. R. (2012). Student flow between community colleges: Investigating lateral transfer. *Research in Higher Education, 53,* 94–121.

Bahr, P. R., Toth, C., Thirolf, K., & Massé, J. C. (2013). A review and critique of the literature on community college students' transition processes and outcomes in four-year institutions. *Higher Education: Handbook of Theory and Research, 28,* 459–511.

Brint, S., & Karabel, J. (1989). *The diverted dream: Community colleges and the promise of educational opportunity in America, 1900–1985.* New York: Oxford University Press.

Deil-Amen, R., & Rosenbaum, J. E. (2003). The social prerequisites of success: Can college structure reduce the need for social know-how? *Annals of the American Academy of Political and Social Science, 586,* 120–143.

Hodara, M., Martinez-Wenzl, M., Stevens, D., & Mazzeo, C. (2016). *Improving credit mobility for community college transfer students: Findings and recommendations from a 10-state study.* Portland, OR: Education Northwest.

Horn, L., & Skomsvold, P. (2011). *Community college student outcomes: 1994–2009* (NCES 2012–253). Washington, DC: U.S. Department of Education, Institute of Education Sciences, National Center for Education Statistics.

Ishitani, T. (2008). How do transfers survive after "transfer shock"? A longitudinal study of transfer student departure at a four-year institution. *Research in Higher Education, 49,* 403–419.

Jenkins, D., Lahr, H., & Fink, J. (2017). *Implementing Guided Pathways: Early Insights from the AACC Pathways Colleges*. New York: Columbia University, Teachers College, Community College Research Center.

Jenkins, D., & Fink, J. (2016). *Tracking transfer: New measures of institutional and state effectiveness in helping community college students attain bachelor's degrees*. New York, NY: Columbia University, Teachers College, Community College Research Center.

Long, B. T., & Kurlaender, M. (2009). Do community colleges provide a viable pathway to a baccalaureate degree? *Educational Evaluation and Policy Analysis, 31*, 30–53.

Millard, M. (2014). *Students on the move: How states are responding to increasing mobility among postsecondary students*. Denver, CO: Education Commission of the States.

Monaghan, D. B., & Attewell, P. (2015). The community college route to the bachelor's degree. *Educational Evaluation and Policy Analysis, 371*, 70–91.

Mullin, C. M. (2012). *Transfer: An indispensable part of the community college mission* (Policy Brief 2012-03PBL). Washington, DC: American Association of Community Colleges.

National Student Clearinghouse Research Center. (2015). *Contribution of two-year institutions to four-year completions* (Snapshot Report). Herndon, VA: National Student Clearinghouse Research Center.

Roska, J. (2006). Does the vocational focus of community colleges hinder students' educational attainment? *Review of Higher Education, 29*(4), 499–526.

Roska, J., & Keith, B. (2008). Credits, time, and attainment: Articulation policies and success after transfer. *Educational Evaluation and Policy Analysis, 303*, 236–254.

Shapiro, D., Dundar, A., Wakhungu, P. K., Yuan, X., & Harrell, A. (2015). *Transfer and mobility: A national view of student movement in postsecondary institutions, Fall 2008 cohort* (Signature Report No. 9). Herndon, VA: National Student Clearinghouse Research Center.

Smith, M. (2010). *Transfer and articulation policies* (State Notes). Denver, CO: Education Commission of the States.

Taylor, J. L. (2015). *Reverse transfer convening: Expanding conversations and surfacing impacts* [Blog post]. Retrieved from http://occrl.illinois.edu/our-products/current-topics-detail/current-topics/2015/06/16/reverse-transfer-convening-expanding-conversations-and-surfacing-impacts

Wyner, J., Deane, K. C., Jenkins, D., & Fink, J. (2016). *The transfer playbook: Essential practices for two- and four-year colleges*. Washington, DC: Aspen Institute.

Christopher A. Baldwin is associate vice president for postsecondary state policy at Jobs for the Future.

5

In this chapter, we discuss how the workforce development mission has evolved over the past 10 years, how the mission plays out at community colleges today, what it may look like in the future, and questions that need to be considered.

Changing the Economy One Family at a Time: Dual Aims of Workforce Development

Regina L. Garza Mitchell, James O. Sawyer, IV

Workforce development (WFD) is an important mission component for most community colleges. Ten years ago Jim Jacobs and Kevin Dougherty (2006) wrote that community colleges had two primary approaches to addressing workforce development: either focusing on the needs of the business sector or on lifting low-income workers. In our view, the best colleges today are attempting to meet both ends: improving socioeconomic conditions for those who need it most by helping displaced and underemployed workers enter the workforce, maintaining open access, and meeting industry needs by providing workforce training that enables employers to develop their businesses and, in turn, to boost the economy through jobs that pay a living wage. Although Jacobs and Dougherty noted that the two ends are not mutually exclusive, they felt "it is difficult to see how even the most comprehensive community college would be able to effectively implement both" (p. 58). It is not easy to navigate these multiple goals and the tensions that arise from them. Meeting these paradoxical objectives exemplifies some of the multiple missions served by community colleges. They are not mutually exclusive, but they are necessary. Being able to balance these multiple missions is even more important in the postrecession economy. Job recovery has been uneven, with those having a high school diploma or less being negatively affected the most (Carnevale, Jayasundera, & Gulish, 2016). Today it is more important than ever that workers earn postsecondary credentials to attain the skills that are required to participate in our current economic recovery.

NEW DIRECTIONS FOR COMMUNITY COLLEGES, no. 180, Winter 2017 © 2017 Wiley Periodicals, Inc.
Published online in Wiley Online Library (wileyonlinelibrary.com) • DOI: 10.1002/cc.20280

In this chapter, we discuss how the workforce development mission has evolved over the past 10 years, how the mission plays out at community colleges today, and what it may look like in the future. We close by posing questions that need to be considered by community college researchers, administrators, and faculty.

Federal and State Context

One key reason for the current emphasis on workforce development stems from President Obama's 2008 speech at Macomb Community College in which he announced the American Graduation Initiative (AGI). He focused on community colleges as a means of increasing the number of Americans holding college credentials by the year 2020 and noted the need to "reform and strengthen community colleges from coast to coast so that they get the resources students and schools need—and the results workers and businesses demand" (White House, 2009, para. 3). The result was a proposed $12 billion in funding for community colleges, primarily focused on workforce development programs and initiatives.

Although the full amount of funding was not provided, the federal government allocated $2 billion as an incentive to increase associate degree and certificate attainment through the Trade Adjustment Assistance Community College and Career Training Grant Program (TAACCCT). The TAACCCT program appropriated between $450 and $500 million each year from 2011 to 2014 to assist colleges in expanding and improving education and training that focused on preparing workers and students for employment in high-wage, high-skill areas (U.S. Department of Labor, 2014). These funds specifically require partnerships with local employers, with the intended outcome of students entering in-demand, high-wage jobs. Particular emphasis was placed on aligning education programs with industry credentials. Thus, this program assists in meeting two goals: student attainment of educational credentials (educational and industry) and economic development of local communities.

Although the full amount of President Obama's proposed funding was never realized, other agencies took up the call of the AGI and focused money and effort on community colleges. Groups with a national impact such as Lumina Foundation's Goal 2025 (https://www.luminafoundation.org/goal_2025), Gates Foundation (http://www.gatesfoundation.org/What-We-Do/US-Program/Postsecondary-Success), and New America (https://www.newamerica.org/asset-building/overcoming-obstacles-to-college-attendance-and-degree-completion/) announced their own calls for increasing the number of college credentials earned by Americans as predictions emerged that future jobs would require skills and degrees not currently held by American adults.

However, even as these national calls for completion were heard, funding for community colleges decreased dramatically. In a 2011 report, 9 out of 10 state community college leaders believed that there were no long-term plans in place to finance the cost of expanding degree completion (Katsinas, D'Amico, & Friedel, 2011). Despite these concerns, many state governments heeded these calls and combined the need for more graduates with the need for rebuilding the economy.

For example, in a special message to the people of Michigan, Governor Rick Snyder (2011) called for talent development, noting that only 35% of adults in the state had college credentials but by 2018 62% of jobs in the state would require a degree. Snyder stated:

> Job growth projections can only be realized if Michigan has the talent to support job providers. While traditional college attainment remains a vital part of our reinvention plan, we must recognize that associate degrees, advanced degrees and vocational credentials play equally important roles. (pp. 3–4)

This statement is significant for several reasons. It reflected the nationwide feeling that Americans desperately need to earn more and different college credentials in order to avoid future economic distress, it focused on community colleges, and it reflected the sentiment that despite its long history and enrolling nearly half of all undergraduates in the country, community college credentials—particularly those in workforce programs—are viewed as nontraditional and of lesser value. Snyder also noted the need for postsecondary education to be both marketable and transferrable, and he went on to say, "State support of postsecondary education should be concentrated in areas that enhance our economic development strategy" (p. 4). Snyder's emphasis on workforce education continued in 2015 with an extension of the Michigan New Jobs Training program, which provides funding for new or expanding businesses to support the cost of training new employees by diverting withheld state income tax to community colleges rather than to the state (Michigan Community College Association, 2016), and in 2016 when the governor pledged a $10 million increase to the Skilled Trades Training Fund to match employees with skilled workers.

The state of Texas defines workforce education as courses and programs that "prepare students for immediate employment or job upgrade within specific occupational categories" (Texas Administrative Code, 1998). Both community colleges and technical colleges provide workforce programs, although they serve slightly different functions. In Texas, community colleges are comprehensive institutions that may include workforce development programs whereas technical colleges, through the Texas State Technical College (TSTC) System, offer only workforce education. The mission statement for the TSTC System states:

> Texas State Technical College System (TSTC) shall contribute to the educational and economic development of the State of Texas by offering occupationally oriented programs with supporting academic course work,

emphasizing highly specialized advanced and emerging technical and vocational areas for certificates or associate degrees. (TSTC, 2016, para. 2)

The emphasis on economic value was further emphasized in 2007 when the state decided to implement performance-based funding measures for higher education. State officials and technical college leaders felt that the technical college system and its students provided economic value to the state and proposed a value-added funding model that was "built on the concept of aligning the state's investment in TSTC with the estimated total economic benefit that comes back to the state in increased tax revenue produced by former students" (Selingo & Van Der Werf, 2016, p. 2). The model is based on income that students earn within 5 years after leaving or graduating from the college, providing they have earned at least nine credit hours from the college. The funding model took effect in the 2014–2015 academic year, so few data are available to date but it does not appear to have had great impact on funding received from the state. It is important to note that the formula does place greater emphasis on the needs of employers and industry demands (Selingo & Van Der Werf); however it also addresses a key issue faced by community colleges in the age of accountability: how to better measure student success when students may only wish to complete a few courses. A key element to this performance formula attempts to measure the outcomes of successful noncompleters rather than focusing solely on credential attainment (Booth & Bahr, 2013).

Available funding from governmental and foundational sources combined with the increased external demand for completion resulted in a visible shift in credentials earned at community colleges, particularly in certificate-level attainment. Between 2000 and 2014, the overall number of certificates awarded by community colleges increased by 236%, with certificates comprising 39% of all community college credentials awarded in 2014 (Phillippe & Tekle, 2016). Despite the increases in both degree and certificate attainment during that period, a 2015 report indicated that productivity was slowing because of cuts in state appropriations after the end of funds from the Recovery Act, cuts to the Pell grant program in 2012, and economic recovery (Katsinas et al., 2015). The report also showed that the majority of states (three out of four) did not have long-term budget plans in place needed for increased degree and certificate attainment. Workforce education is expensive, as is the cost of supporting students through completion of a credential. Without solid plans for funding in place at both federal (student aid) and state (appropriations), the future of workforce education is called into question. Colleges cannot continue to develop and provide workforce education programs that integrate skills and credentials employers require without a sustainable funding model.

Transferability and Partnerships

The very nature of workforce development requires colleges to work closely with local industry in ensuring existing and new programs are relevant to local needs. For many years workforce programs were equated with training rather than education. Although the differences may be slight, workforce programs are typically offered as either certificate programs or applied associate degrees, neither of which was typically able to transfer toward further education or a baccalaureate degree. The past 10 years, however, have seen an increase in credit for prior learning, noncredit to credit transfer, transferability of applied degrees, and competency-based courses through state initiatives and partnerships.

It is important to recognize that a great deal of learning takes place outside the classroom. Colleges need to have processes to capture and give credit to students for what they have learned. Many colleges have credit for prior learning processes that are used to award credit based on successfully passing tests, earning industry certifications, or submitting portfolios for faculty review. Converting noncredit training programs to college credit is an emerging alternative method for acknowledging this type of adult learning. Noncredit to credit conversion requires alignment between the programs. Workforce training programs become an effective way to demonstrate to students they can complete college-level work. The idea is that once students experience success in college and have already earned some college credit, they become motivated to further their education. Because participants in workforce programs are often lower skilled and receive lower compensation, the awarding of credit for training programs becomes a great on-ramp to further their education and increase earned wages.

Transferability of applied associate degrees has become particularly important because of the growing demand for baccalaureate degrees. Carnevale, Smith, and Strohl (2013) project that by 2020 65% of jobs will require postsecondary education, with 35% of jobs requiring at least a baccalaureate degree. As the demand for baccalaureate degrees increases, particularly in science, technology, engineering, and mathematics and healthcare professions, it is important that associate degrees in those fields serve as entry points into baccalaureate programs. Encouraging transfer in this manner also opens options for students in workforce fields, which, in the past, were closed beyond the associate degree.

In Michigan, some universities are starting to accept applied associate degree programs to transfer to baccalaureate programs. Associate-level nursing degree programs, for example, are now transferring to baccalaureate nursing programs. This is important because hospitals increasingly require baccalaureate-educated nurses for entry-level positions. Another recent evolution is the acceptance of credit earned in traditional skilled trades programs being accepted toward baccalaureate degrees. One example is applied technology courses at Macomb Community College being accepted for transfer into several engineering technology programs at Wayne State University.

The rise of competency-based education has brought challenges and benefits to workforce education. The format allows greater flexibility in the way that credentials are earned and allows learning to be personalized. The faculty role transcends the traditional sage-on-the-stage dissemination model to a model in which faculty facilitate learning for each individual student. The facilitation model recognizes that students, particularly older students with work and life experiences, progress through material at their own pace as they learn key concepts, moving from lower level competencies to higher level learning. Colleges have engaged in this type of education for years, primarily on the noncredit side. With the shift to competency-based education as a credit-bearing mechanism, the possibility exists for students who work to have an alternative route to earning a degree.

For example, Central Maine Technical College has implemented a competency-based Certificate in Advanced Machining that allows students who already have an associate degree (or equivalent) in machining to earn the degree at their own pace through a combination of online courses and individual lab time. The program was developed through a National Science Foundation Advanced Technological Education (ATE) Grant (http://www.cmcc.edu/ramp/CertificateinAdvancedMachining.aspx#.V0RP ImbLPfB). Didactic coursework is done online, and students complete course projects in labs on campus by reserving a lab station when they are ready. The competency-based approach meets the needs of working students and of employers who need employees with advanced skills, and it alleviates the issue of limited lab space. The college partnered with local employers, other colleges, and other ATE centers to develop curriculum and serve students. A key outcome is that students who have completed an associate degree and the advanced certificate can then transfer to a partnering university and complete a baccalaureate degree within a year (Dosti, 2016, personal communication). This type of program is an example of how colleges attempt to meet the needs of students and employers. Although Central Maine Technical College has implemented this program, competency-based education is still a relatively new phenomenon that has not yet been fully embraced by the educational community.

The transferability of applied programs is critical for two key reasons. First, it allows students who traditionally may not have been ready or able to move into further education to pursue it, if they choose, in the future. Second, employers are increasingly emphasizing baccalaureate degrees. Baccalaureate degrees may be favored over associate degrees because the additional education, typically in nontechnical areas (i.e., general education), provides an opportunity to enhance a student's ability to further develop employability and workplace skills such as critical thinking, problem solving, and communication. There is a greater emphasis on contextualizing education in a meaningful way and better blending it with general education. The emphasis on technical transfer for further education is helping in this regard and may be a solution to the highly touted dilemma of workplace skills.

Changing Families

WFD has been associated primarily with training and economic development. Jacobs and Dougherty (2006) noted that colleges have a choice between two paths in regard to workforce development: new vocationalism, which prepares students for further education in the field rather than entry-level jobs, or workforce development for low-income workers, which views community colleges as institutions that can lift low-income workers out of poverty. The emphasis overall seems to remain focused on skills training and attaining a job as an end goal. Although it is challenging, we feel that the workforce development mission can and should target multiple aims, including preparing students for further education and being engaged citizens.

Workforce education is often viewed as a "dead end" for students (e.g., Rhoades, 2012), and it is up to college leaders and faculty to dispel this myth by ensuring student learning is key and transfer opportunities expand. Colleges need to develop clear pathways, including both academic and workforce programming, so students are able to understand the possibilities that exist (Bailey, Jaggars, & Jenkins, 2015). Students must be able to track their progress along the pathway to help encourage them to complete a program. Colleges need to integrate credentials and alternative forms of credit attainment, including credit earned at other institutions, into the pathways. Through increased transfer pathways for applied degrees and certificates, opportunities are opening up for students to continue their education and earn higher level degrees. Although that may not be the choice for everyone, providing the opportunity represents a significant shift in how workforce education is viewed and ensures students are not being terminally "cooled out" if they want to move on.

We who work (or have worked) at community colleges view WFD as an opportunity to change families. Students who participate in workforce programs are often unemployed or underemployed. These students are interested in obtaining the skills necessary to secure immediate employment. There is nothing more important or rewarding that community colleges do than help people improve their family's economic status. This benefits not only the family but also the community. Being gainfully employed not only reduces reliance on public assistance, it also enables individuals to contribute to the economic well-being of their community.

Skills development—technical and workplace—must be aligned with traditional academic values to ensure students who enter the workforce have the skills desired by employers and those they need to progress. Simply learning technical skills, which is how workforce training programs used to be designed, is no longer acceptable. In response to feedback from employers in all sectors, Macomb has started to integrate teaching workplace skills into technical training programs. Employers make it clear that technical skills are important, but if employees do not have workplace skills such as critical thinking, problem solving, communication, and work ethic, they will not be successful in their organization.

Community colleges are known for attempting to serve multiple audiences and missions, but the demands continue to increase. As funding levels decline, colleges are having to make difficult decisions in regard to curriculum and often find themselves chasing the money in order to fund expensive programs, such as those that require laboratory space and equipment. As workforce programs are created, enhanced, and refined, student needs must be kept in mind while meeting the numerous other demands. In particular, colleges must remain focused on improving workforce education to account for both economic ends and student growth and learning (Harbour & Wolgemouth, 2015).

References

Bailey, T. R., Jaggars, S. S., & Jenkins, D. (2015). *Redesigning America's community colleges: A clearer path to student success.* Cambridge, MA: Harvard University Press.

Booth, K., & Bahr, P. R. (2013). *The missing piece: Quantifying non-completion pathways to success.* Oakland, CA: LearningWorks. Retrieved from http://www.learning worksca.org/the-missing-piece/

Carnevale, A. P., Jayasundera, T., & Gulish, A. (2016). *America's divided recovery: College haves and have-nots.* Washington, DC: Georgetown University, McCourt School of Public Policy, Center on Education and the Workforce.

Carnevale, A. P., Smith, N., & Strohl, J. (2013). *Recovery: Job growth and education requirements through 2020.* Washington, DC: Georgetown University, Center on Education and the Workforce, Georgetown Public Policy Institute.

Harbour, C. P., & Wolgemouth, J. R. (2015). The reconstruction of community college vocational education: A vision for renewing America's democracy. *Community College Review, 43*(4), 315–328. https://doi.org/10.1177/0091552115580391

Jacobs, J., & Dougherty, K. J. (2006). The uncertain future of the community college workforce development mission. In B. K. Townsend & K. J. Dougherty (Eds.), *New Directions for Community Colleges: No. 136. Community college missions in the twenty-first century* (pp. 53–62). San Francisco, CA: Jossey-Bass. https://doi.org/10.1002/cc.259

Katsinas, S. G., D'Amico, M. M., & Friedel, J. N. (2011). *Challenging success: Can college degree completion be increased as states cut budgets?* Tuscaloosa, AL: University of Alabama Education Policy Center. Retrieved from http://www.public.iastate.edu/~jfriedel/pubs/College%20Completion%202011%20 11-12-2011.pdf

Katsinas, S. G., Shedd, L. E., Malley, M. S., Adair, J. L., D'Amico, M. M., & Friedel, J. N. (2015). *A new way forward is needed to jump start degree completion.* Tuscaloosa, AL: University of Alabama Education Policy Center.

Michigan Community College Association. (2016). *What is the Michigan New Jobs Training Program?* Retrieved from http://www.mcca.org/content.cfm?ID=43

Phillippe, K., & Tekle, R. (2016, January). Boom in certificates. *Data Points.* Retrieved from http://www.aacc.nche.edu/Publications/datapoints/Documents/DP_Jan7.pdf

Rhoades, G. (2012). The incomplete completion agenda: Implications for academe and the academy. *Liberal Education, 98*(1), 18–25. Retrieved from http://www.aacu.org/publications-research/periodicals/incomplete-completion-agenda-implications-acade me-and-academy

Selingo, J. J., & Van Der Werf, M. (2016, March). *Linking appropriations for the Texas State Technical College System to student employment outcomes.* Indianapolis, IN: Lumina Foundation. Retrieved from https://www.luminafoundation.org/resources/linking-appropriations-for-the-texas-state-technical-college-system-to-student-employment-outcomes

Snyder, R. (2011). *A special message from Governor Rick Snyder: Developing and connecting Michigan's talent.* Retrieved from http://www.michigan.gov/documents/snyder/SpecialMessageonTalent_369995_7.pdf

Texas Administrative Code, Title 19, Part 1, Chapter 11, Subchapter A, Rule §11.3 (1998). Retrieved from http://txrules.elaws.us/rule/title19_chapter11_sec.11.3

Texas State Technical College. (2016). *Mission.* Retrieved from http://www.tstc.edu/about/mission

U. S. Department of Labor. (2014). *Trade Adjustment Assistance Community College and Career Grant Training Program.* Retrieved from https://doleta.gov/taaccct/

White House. (2009, July 14). *Excerpts of the President's remarks in Warren, Michigan, and fact sheet on the American Graduation Initiative.* Retrieved from https://obamawhitehouse.archives.gov/the-press-office/excerpts-presidents-remarks-warren-michigan-and-fact-sheet-american-graduation-init

REGINA L. GARZA MITCHELL *is associate professor of higher education leadership in the Educational Leadership, Research, and Technology department at Western Michigan University.*

JAMES O. SAWYER IV *is president of Macomb Community College.*

NEW DIRECTIONS FOR COMMUNITY COLLEGES • DOI: 10.1002/cc

6

This chapter discusses an often neglected aspect of the community college mission: noncredit courses that address local service area needs.

Noncredit Education: Specialized Programs to Meet Local Needs

Mark M. D'Amico

Although preparing the workforce is a key duty for community colleges, there is one primary delivery mechanism that is often overlooked: non-credit education. According to the National Center for Education Statistics (NCES, 2016), a noncredit course is "A course or activity having no credit applicable toward a degree, diploma, certificate, or other formal award" (p. 22). The American Association of Community Colleges (2017a) reports that community colleges enroll 5 million noncredit students each year. Despite the prevalence and evolution of the noncredit role, recent discussions of the changing mission have involved topics such as baccalaureate degrees (Floyd & Walker, 2009), honors programs (Treat & Barnard, 2012), and diversity and culture (Andrade & Lundberg, 2016). There has been little attention to the aspect of the mission that represents 40% of community college headcount enrollment. Voorhees and Milam (2005) referred to noncredit as the "hidden college." Van Noy, Jacobs, Korey, Bailey, and Hughes (2008) described how the noncredit mission is even separated organizationally within many community colleges.

The purpose of this chapter is to describe the noncredit environment and the primary functions of noncredit education in community colleges as they work to meet local needs.

The Noncredit Environment

Although they provide important training services for individuals and businesses in local areas, noncredit courses and programs receive less attention than their for-credit counterparts for several reasons. The first is funding, because state-level funding is not available in all states (see, for example, Oleksiw, Kremidas, Johnson-Lewis, & Lekes, 2007; Van Noy et al., 2008; Voorhees & Milam, 2005). State funding can provide motivation to enhance

NEW DIRECTIONS FOR COMMUNITY COLLEGES, no. 180, Winter 2017 © 2017 Wiley Periodicals, Inc.
Published online in Wiley Online Library (wileyonlinelibrary.com) • DOI: 10.1002/cc.20281

noncredit offerings, but it may also influence the way offerings are selected. For example, colleges may elect not to offer noncredit courses for state reimbursement if it means controls on tuition. Colleges that offer noncredit education as a completely self-supported enterprise may set tuition according to what the market will bear; thus, noncredit can be viewed as a revenue generator, while addressing local needs.

Another reason for the "hidden" status is accountability. Because many states do not fund noncredit offerings, colleges are often not required to report on noncredit as a part of accountability mandates (see, for example, Oleksiw et al., 2007; Van Noy et al., 2008; Voorhees & Milam, 2005). However, that may be changing. One of the federal funding sources for noncredit training in community colleges is the Workforce Innovation and Opportunity Act (WIOA) (U.S. Department of Labor Employment and Training Administration, 2014). With implementation of the legislation, there are performance indicators, which will need to be reported for participating noncredit programs. It is important to note, however, that colleges may choose not to participate in WIOA because of the reporting requirements. Additionally, the American Association of Community Colleges' (2017bb) Voluntary Framework for Accountability (VFA) includes noncredit career and technical education (CTE) outcome measures for participating institutions and states to track.

Meeting Local Needs

In many states, the primary driver of noncredit enrollment is occupational education to meet the unique needs of business and industry. Local needs are drivers of for-credit CTE offerings, but noncredit education provides the greatest flexibility to develop and implement programs, in many cases without the scrutiny of oversight beyond institutional approvals. Thus, noncredit delivery allows nimble colleges to ramp up offerings to meet the needs of individuals and employers. This workforce development mechanism is typically delivered through open enrollment occupational training and sponsored (contract) training, especially considering key local economic development priorities. According to *Area Development's* (2015) survey of site selection consultants, availability of skilled labor is the second highest ranked site selection factor for businesses looking to expand or relocate operations. Thus, the education provided in a market, which may include noncredit education, is important to state/regional/local economic development when partnering with community colleges to provide site location incentives to corporations.

The noncredit function is not entirely about training in CTE areas, however. Noncredit is also a key delivery mechanism for adult education (General Educational Development [GED], English as a second language, etc.). According to the U.S. Department of Education (2016), approximately 15 states have a higher education agency (most often community or technical college systems) as the designated state adult education agency. Also, many other states' community colleges partner with departments of education and labor and state coordinating bodies to deliver adult education services at low or no cost to students, thus not requiring Pell grant use or other aid. Unlike the typical developmental education offerings in community colleges, which do not yield college-level credit but are still offered through credit-based structures and reported to the Integrated Postsecondary Education Data System each year, the GED, English as a second language (ESL), and adult basic education (ABE) functions are often delivered through noncredit formats.

These noncredit functions are chronicled in the many labels used in the community college literature: continuing education, workforce education, lifelong learning, personal enrichment, workforce instruction, contract training, community service, community-based education, and many others (see, for example, Oleksiw et al., 2007; Van Noy et al., 2008; Voorhees & Milam, 2005). Although noncredit education may not be a new delivery mechanism for community colleges, it is underemphasized in discussions partially because of a lack of consistent terminology and understanding. In an effort to clarify the key functions of noncredit enrollment, D'Amico, Morgan, Robertson, and Houchins (2014) analyzed the headcount enrollment of one state's noncredit enrollment to devise a categorization of noncredit course types. They include "occupational training," "sponsored occupational (contract) training," "personal interest," and "pre-college remediation" (p. 157).

Noncredit Types

Each of the noncredit types provides community colleges with mechanisms to meet the needs of specific constituents in their regions, including individuals seeking to obtain new skills, organizations intending to upskill their workforce, community members engaging in enriching experiences, or those pursuing precollege programs. The following sections describe the noncredit types with examples of how community colleges are addressing local demand.

Occupational Training. Noncredit occupational training is geared toward individuals seeking to gain or improve job skills leading to initial or better employment. These courses are most often available through an open registration process, do not follow a typical semester schedule, and are paid for by individuals through either their own resources or through third-party funding for which they are eligible (for example: WIOA, vocational rehabilitation, veterans' benefits). The cost varies based on program area, course or program duration, and the availability of state subsidies. For example, a 30-hour welding course may cost several hundred dollars plus equipment because of instructor and facility expenses, whereas an online course in web design yielding a similar number of continuing education units (CEUs) may be one third the cost. In addition to CEUs earned through noncredit courses, many may lead to industry-recognized credentials through completion and/or an exam. Although these are often seen in areas such as manufacturing or information technology, other certifications such as a Commercial Driver's License are available through noncredit.

Another important noncredit consideration is the variety of students who enroll. Some courses could enroll individuals without a high school diploma and have those with professional degrees in the same class. These courses, especially if not subsidized, are offered based on individual and industry demand, which results in strong linkages to local workforce needs.

An example is Kirkwood Community College in Cedar Rapids, Iowa, and its use of noncredit education to address regional manufacturing needs in welding. Iowa has experienced significant growth in manufacturing since 2010, nearly 7,000 new jobs (Elevate Advanced Manufacturing, n.d.). Through an initiative of the Iowa-Advanced Manufacturing (I-AM) project funded with the U.S. Department of Labor Trade Adjustment Assistance Community College Career Training (TAACCCT) grant, the college developed a pathway that begins with recruitment, assessment, and enrollment phases, leading to a bridge course followed by the noncredit offerings in welding. The noncredit welding credential then articulates into the credit-based program. Another key component of the project is that tuition and other expenses are covered for eligible students through the state-funded PACE (Pathways for Academic Career and Employment) Program. Sixty-eight students have been served through 2016 (K. Becicka, personal communication, August 30, 2016).

Addressing a very different purpose, community colleges have demonstrated their adaptability by preparing individuals for the growing craft brewing industry. This is seen in North Carolina with the industry's $1.2 billion in economic impact and a 173% increase in the number of breweries from 2011 to 2015 (Brewers Association, 2016). Because of the need for qualified workers in western North Carolina, Asheville-Buncombe Technical Community College (n.d.) in Asheville offers both credit and noncredit training through the Craft Beverage Institute of the Southeast. Courses are developed and delivered to those seeking positions, as well as those moving forward in their careers. Blue Ridge Community College (2014), also in western North Carolina, delivers noncredit continuing education instruction through their Craft Beer Academy. Blue Ridge is one of three examination centers in North Carolina for the General Certificate in Brewing, a credential offered by the Institute of Brewing & Distilling. Similarly, Oregon with its $1.8 billion in economic impact and the number two ranking in breweries per capita (Brewers Association, 2016) presents numerous employment opportunities. Central Oregon Community College (2016) in Bend, Oregon, addresses that need with its General Certificate in Brewing (GCB) Exam Prep Course, which prepares individuals to pursue the industry-recognized credential.

Sponsored Occupational (Contract) Training.   Sponsored noncredit training is similar to the occupational training described previously with one key difference. It is arranged by special contract with organizations, which include private and public, and for profit and not for profit. Sponsored noncredit training can be specific training developed for an organization, or it can lead to some particular industry-based standard. These courses are delivered in a way most convenient for the contracting organization. Payment for training often comes from the contracting organization but could also be captured through a government-funded economic development training mechanism. In each case, contract training responds directly to local area needs and varies by region.

Since 2014, Piedmont Technical College in South Carolina has been engaged in a partnership with ZF Transmissions to deliver instruction to individuals in the company's registered apprenticeship program. Corporation/college partnerships are a priority of the South Carolina Technical College System, and, in recent years, partnerships around registered apprenticeships have intensified. Through the sustained effort of Apprenticeship Carolina (n.d.), South Carolina colleges have served more than 16,000 apprentices in targeted industry clusters. Piedmont Technical College's partnership with ZF Transmissions has led to nearly 100 apprentices trained with the employer paying tuition for the related technical instruction. Additionally, the noncredit computer numerical control (CNC) machine operations offerings are structured to articulate into the machine tool technology associate's degree, thus creating an educational and career pathway (R. Denning, personal communication, August 29, 2016).

The apprenticeship example at Piedmont Technical College directly responds to a manufacturing company's needs and reflects an expected contract training arrangement. However, another example from South Carolina demonstrates how noncredit contract training can occur with a diverse array of partners. In 2015, Midlands Technical College in Columbia, South Carolina, partnered with Richland County School District Two through the Richland 2 Institute of Innovation (R2i2), which works with businesses to prepare students for emerging employment opportunities. Through the initiative, Midlands Technical College delivered courses in Swift Programming and Mobile App Development on their campus, within school district boundaries. Although CEUs were awarded, perhaps the more valued outcome was that the class of high school students each developed an app to be made available in the Apple App Store (B. Kirk, personal communication, August 29, 2016).

Personal Interest.   Personal interest is the least prevalent noncredit course type in terms of enrollment. Common examples include ballroom dancing, cake decorating, and the like. Despite the fact that courses in cake decorating can lead to employment, one concern with such classes is that state dollars are being used support something that does not result in jobs. However, personal interest courses typically do not receive state subsidies for enrollment, yet support local community interests, reinforce community engagement with the college, and may even contribute to economic development efforts. Additionally, as self-supporting courses, personal interest courses are demand driven, because students likely self-pay, and often reflect the needs, interests, and priorities of local communities—one of the key missions of community colleges.

One notable example is Yakima Valley College (YVC) in Yakima, Washington. Through their self-supported (nonsubsidized) community education courses, they address the interests relevant to their service area (Yakima Valley College, 2015). The basic mountaineer course serves a region with more than 400 climbing routes and is in close proximity to Mt. Rainier and Mt. Adams, and courses in beginning and intermediate fly fishing address demand for skills needed to enjoy 109 lakes and 65 miles of the Yakima River (New Vision, 2015; Yakima Valley College, 2015). The YVC courses were once delivered as for-credit offerings but are now noncredit and scheduled only when there is local demand. The instructors, who are familiar with the region's outdoor opportunities, often serve as both recruiter and teacher to ensure that offerings meet enrollment thresholds necessary to cover costs (R. Funk, personal communication, December 7, 2016).

Precollege Remediation.   Finally, precollege remediation is a significant part of the noncredit community college mission; however, its prevalence within colleges depends on the institution and the state policy environment. In the 15 states where higher education entities are the adult education providers recognized by the U.S. Department of Education, the role may be more significant. In other states, where adult education and high school completion are run through K–12 state departments of education and labor departments, the role may be less prominent depending on the presence of interagency partnerships. Within this noncredit function, some of the primary programs delivered include ABE, ESL instruction, GED preparation, and even some aspects of developmental studies. These are typically offered at no charge to the student other than testing fees, supplies, etc.

Although precollege remediation is often delivered on campus, one example demonstrates the flexibility that community colleges exhibit through noncredit offerings. National Park College in Hot Springs, Arkansas, is a provider of noncredit ABE, GED preparation, and ESL classes. In July 2015, the college engaged in a partnership with the Garland County Sheriff's Department to deliver educational services to inmates at the Garland County Detention Center. The impetus of this partnership was the implementation of a county sales tax to fund a new detention center that was better equipped to accommodate educational opportunities in an effort to reduce recidivism. Funding for the adult education offerings comes from federal and state grants administered through the Arkansas Department of Career Education. In the first year of the partnership (2015–2016), National Park College served 509 students resulting in increases in educational functioning among 170 program participants; 19 earned GED diplomas; and the college awarded 150 workforce training certificates (B. Ritter, personal communication, August 12, 2016).

Conclusions

Evident in the examples provided in this chapter are four key elements across noncredit programs. The first is region and industry specificity, as seen through the emerging focus on craft brewing in both North Carolina and Oregon leading to industry-recognized credentials, the South Carolina registered apprenticeship example by offering employer-specific sponsored training, and personal interest courses improving the outdoor experiences of those in the Yakima Valley. As community colleges embrace their local service mission, noncredit is an important vehicle.

The second is funding flexibility. Although there are elements of this in all examples, there is great variation in funding arrangements. The Midlands Technical College partnership with the local school district demonstrates how the partner district funded an experience in app development. The ZF Transmissions example at Piedmont Technical College shows how a business pays for its apprentices to gain related technical instruction. The Yakima Valley Community College community education, Kirkwood Community College welding, North Carolina brewing, and National Park College's adult education examples show how occupational training, personal interest, and/or adult education offerings are funded through a variety of methods including self-pay, student benefit funded, or directly paid by government subsidies. The overarching point is that creative community college leaders have the flexibility to fund noncredit education through a variety of methods to meet local needs.

The third is meeting needs where they exist in local communities. A notable example is National Park College's delivery of services at the Garland County Detention Center. With special avenues of funding for many noncredit offerings, classes can be taught anywhere, anytime, and do not necessarily need to be offered through open enrollment.

The final characteristic of noncredit education is the emergence of stackable credentials through noncredit-to-credit articulation, thus promoting pipelines to higher level skills, certifications, and postsecondary completion. Though not yet common (Van Noy et al., 2008), noncredit-to-credit articulation is an evolving part of the noncredit mission and contradictory to the NCES definition of noncredit. The examples at Kirkwood Community College and Piedmont Technical College demonstrate a more progressive mission for technical programs such as welding and CNC machining, through which a college's commitment to noncredit articulation can lead to creating innovative pathways.

In addition to the themes that emerge among programs, building a general understanding around the four key noncredit types could be used to compare outcomes of noncredit students within appropriate categories. Although literature on noncredit outcomes is not yet common, the expectation is that noncredit student outcomes will be measured with greater frequency with the availability of data through the new WIOA performance measures and VFA implementation.

From a practical perspective, the four course types help to explain the different ways that colleges meet their mission through noncredit education. Occupational training can enhance job skills in a nearly limitless number of areas; sponsored training can serve industries like manufacturing; personal interest courses allow for reflection on the needs of local communities; and precollege remediation can serve individuals where they are.

Based on the many implications of noncredit community college education, the following are recommendations for institutional leaders:

- Consider the college's specific region and the ability to provide offerings to meet unique regional needs in many cases with less oversight and accountability
- Take advantage of partnership opportunities when there are community-wide social service and/or economic development initiatives
- Consider the wide variety of funding avenues (for example, self-pay, student benefits such as WIOA eligibility, employer contracts, state-funded priorities)
- Identify opportunities for career pathways that extend through noncredit offerings to credit programs
- Capture data on noncredit student populations and completion, employment, and wage outcomes when possible
- Use the noncredit types to help explain noncredit functions to constituents

For those who work in or with community colleges, perhaps a better understanding of the noncredit community college mission helps to demystify this segment of program delivery and to expand what is possible as noncredit education receives greater attention. Ultimately, the community college mission is about meeting local needs, and the noncredit function is situated to serve the unique needs of local communities today.

References

American Association of Community Colleges. (2017a). 2017 fact sheet. Washington, DC: Author. Retrieved from http://www.aacc.nche.edu/AboutCC/Pages/fastfactsfactsheet.aspx
American Association of Community Colleges. (2017b). Voluntary framework of accountability metrics manual version 5.0. Washington, DC: Author. Retrieved from http://vfa.aacc.nche.edu/Documents/VFAMetricsManual.pdf
Andrade, L. M., & Lundberg, C. A. (2016). The function to serve: A social-justice-oriented investigation of community college mission statements. Journal of His-

panic Higher Education. Advance online publication. https://doi.org/10.1177/1538192
716653503

Apprenticeship Carolina. (n.d.). *By the numbers*. Columbia, SC: Author. Retrieved from
http://www.apprenticeshipcarolina.com/by-the-numbers.html

Area Development Magazine. (2015, Q1). *11th annual consultants; survey: Consultants'
exhibit confidence and increasing project activity*. Westbury, NY: Author. Retrieved from
http://www.areadevelopment.com/Corporate-Consultants-Survey-Results/Q1-2015/
11th-site-selection-consultants-corporate-RE-survey-8802177.shtml

Asheville-Buncombe Technical Community College. (n.d.). *Craft Beverage Institute
of the Southeast*®. Asheville, NC: Author. Retrieved from https://www.abtech.
edu/sites/default/files/Library/cbi_executive_summary_2014.pdf

Blue Ridge Community College. (2014). *Craft beer academy and classes*. Flat Rock, NC:
Author. Retrieved from http://www.blueridge.edu/craftbeer

Brewers Association. (2016). *State craft beer sales & production statistics, 2016*. Boulder,
CO: Author. Retrieved from https://www.brewersassociation.org/statistics/by-state/

Central Oregon Community College. (2016). *General certificate in brewing
(GCB) exam prep course*. Bend, OR: Author. Retrieved from https://www.cocc.
edu/continuinged/general-certificate-in-brewing-(gcb)-exam-prep-course/

D'Amico, M. M., Morgan, G. B., Robertson, S., & Houchins, C. (2014). An exploration
of noncredit community college enrollment. *Journal of Continuing Higher Education*,
62, 152–162.

Elevate Advanced Manufacturing. (n.d.). *Facts about Iowa manufacturing*. Retrieved from
http://www.elevateiowa.com/iowa-manufacturing/

Floyd, D. L., & Walker, K. P. (2009). The community college baccalaureate: Putting the
pieces together. *Community College Journal of Research and Practice*, 33, 90–124.

National Center for Education Statistics. (2016). *IPEDS 2016–2017 data collection system: 2016–2017 survey materials: Glossary*. Washington, DC: Author. Retrieved from
https://surveys.nces.ed.gov/ipeds/Downloads/Forms/IPEDSGlossary.pdf

New Vision. (2015). *Outdoor recreation*. Yakima, WA: Yakima County Development Cor-
poration. Retrieved from http://www.liveyakimavalley.com/activities/outdoors.html

Oleksiw, C. A., Kremidas, C. C., Johnson-Lewis, M., & Lekes, N. (2007). *Community
college noncredit occupational programming: A study of state policies and funding*. St.
Paul, MN: National Research Center for Career and Technical Education.

Treat, T., & Barnard, T. C. (2012). Seeking legitimacy: The community college mission and the honors college. *Community College Journal of Research and Practice*, 36,
695–712.

U.S. Department of Education. (2016). *State contacts*. Washington, DC: Author. Retrieved from http://www2.ed.gov/about/contacts/state/index.html

U.S. Department of Labor Employment and Training Administration. (2014).
WIOA fact sheet. Washington, DC: Author. Retrieved from https://www.doleta.gov/
wioa/Docs/WIOA_Factsheets.pdf

Van Noy, M., Jacobs, J., Korey, S., Bailey, T., & Hughes, K. L. (2008). *Noncredit
enrollment in workforce education: State policies and community college practices*.
Washington, DC: American Association of Community Colleges. Retrieved from
http://www.aacc.nche.edu/Publications/Reports/Documents/noncredit.pdf

Voorhees, R. A., & Milam, J. H. (2005). *The hidden college: Noncredit education in the United States*. Retrieved from http://www.voorheesgroup.org/
voorheesgroup-pubs/Hidden%20College.pdf

Yakima Valley College. (2015). *Community classes*. Yakima, WA: Author. Retrieved from
https://www.yvcc.edu/academics/cont-ed/Pages/GoldCard.aspx

MARK M. D'AMICO *is associate professor of educational leadership (higher education) in the department of Educational Leadership, The University of North Carolina at Charlotte.*

NEW DIRECTIONS FOR COMMUNITY COLLEGES • DOI: 10.1002/cc

7

This chapter addresses the impact of free community college and state merit scholarships on college-going patterns of high school graduates, community college revenue contexts, and student access and completion at community colleges.

Free Community College and Merit Scholarships

Lori Elliott Buchanan, Kristin Bailey Wilson

Community college enrollments have waxed and waned throughout their history, and persistence/graduation rates are stubbornly low. Nonetheless, community colleges are places of democratic opportunity. Americans look to community colleges to provide the educational opportunities that change lives, as do business, political, and educational leaders. Increasing educational opportunities for Americans is a mission that is ageless. One policy mechanism that addresses the community college's social and local mission of access is merit scholarships. Typically, these are government grants awarded to students for academic achievement. Often, the grant funding is available only to students attending certain types of colleges, namely public community colleges.

Merit scholarships are frequently billed as free community college to high school graduates. Many states offer some version of merit aid couched as free community college (e.g., Missouri's A+ Schools, Tennessee Promise), and past federal administrations have broached the idea. For example, the Obama administration proposed a program titled *America's College Promise* (2015) that included free community college. However, the possible unintended consequences of this strategy have been largely ignored. Wholesale free college is a move away from providing need-based grants and scholarships directed toward low-income students. The result may be increased stratification in higher education (Bergerson, 2009). This is particularly true when considering the effectiveness of the residential college in graduating students. Given the increasing popularity of free college and the need to explore its unintended consequences, free community college and state merit aid are important aspects of examining the evolving multiple missions of community colleges.

New Directions for Community Colleges, no. 180, Winter 2017 © 2017 Wiley Periodicals, Inc.
Published online in Wiley Online Library (wileyonlinelibrary.com) • DOI: 10.1002/cc.20282

Completion

Increasing completion is crucial for the United States' future economic and social viability. Moreover, each individual's social and economic mobility hinges on completing college. Internationally, the U.S. college completion rate has declined and the proportion of young adults with an associate degree has declined in comparison to other developed countries (Field, 2015). Given the need to increase college completion, federal and state officials are looking to community colleges to enroll more students and produce additional transfer students and associate degree graduates.

Financial Aid and Debt

Since the Higher Education Act of 1965 was passed, the "average aid per student more than tripled, from $3,437 to $12,455 (in constant 2010 dollars)" (Dynarski & Scott-Clayton, 2013, p. 68). In 2010–2011, $190 billion ($147 billion local, state, and federal dollars) were delivered to undergraduates. Almost every student expects and is offered some form of financial assistance. Yet, according to estimates by the Federal Reserve Bank of New York, student loan debt hovers around 1.1 trillion dollars and represents 42 million borrowers (Looney & Yannelis, 2015). Low-income and ethnic/racial minority students carry the heaviest amount of debt; however, two thirds of all students have student loan debt.

Free Community College Programs and State Merit Aid Programs. The first state merit scholarship program was introduced in Arkansas in 1991. This program contributed $2,500 per year toward tuition costs at Arkansas public 2-year and 4-year institutions for eligible high school students who achieved the required grade point average (GPA) of 2.5 or better and an ACT score of 19 or better (Domina, 2014; Dynarski, 2004). Using the generosity levels of such programs, Domina (2014) described and categorized 24 current state merit aid programs. Four states were deemed to be very generous, "fully fund[ing] in-state tuition and fees plus an allowance for educational expenses for students who enrolled" at a state public institution, or "the equivalent amount for students who enroll in one of the state's private colleges or universities" (p. 4). Eight states promised to cover full tuition costs at public institutions. The remaining 10 states provided "less than in-state tuition, with aid amounts that are capped at a fixed dollar level or a fixed proportion of in-state tuition levels" (p. 4). In the case of New Mexico, students qualified for aid when they earned a GPA of 2.5 or better during their first full-time semesters at the state's public institutions (Domina, 2014; Dynarski, 2004).

Ten more states are considering comparable legislation (National Conference of State Legislatures, 2016). As Romano and Palmer (2016) note, these programs "are really 'last dollar' scholarship programs for high school graduates designed to cover tuition and fees after federal and state aid have been applied" (p. 127). "First dollar" programs, such as the proposed America's College Promise, do not consider Pell Grants and other grant funding, whereas "last dollar" programs address any remaining dollars toward tuition beyond that funded through Pell Grants and other grant funding. The Pell Grant covers the cost of most community colleges, so last dollar programs do not typically benefit low-income students despite being cast as a program that helps the disadvantaged.

Changing College-Going Patterns of High School Graduates

To better understand potential unintended consequences, an examination of how free community college and state merit aid change college-going patterns of high school graduates follows.

Merit Scholarships.   Researchers are interested in how merit aid policy adjustments affect college-going patterns of students (Ingle & Ratliff, 2015; Ness 2008; Ness & Noland, 2007; Page & Scott-Clayton, 2016). Although single-state studies comprise a large share of research about merit scholarships, the number of cross-state research studies is growing. These findings suggest answers to whether or not free community college and merit aid programs change college-going patterns of high school graduates.

Several researchers submit that state merit scholarships

- increase college enrollments, and do so at a faster rate compared with states who do not provide this type of aid
- lead to more students attending colleges in their home states
- result in higher enrollments when restricted to public colleges
- extend access when part-time enrollment is permitted (Cornwell, Mustard, & Sridhar, 2006; Domina, 2014; Dynarski & Scott-Clayton, 2013; Farrell & Kienzl, 2009; Muñoz, Harrington, Curs, & Ehlert, 2016; Toutkoushian & Hillman, 2012; Zhang, Hu, & Sensenig, 2013)

Examining research covering some of the larger state-level programs, Dynarski and Scott-Clayton (2013) demonstrate that "an additional $1,000 grant aid may increase college enrollment by 4 percentage points" (p. 79). Several researchers affirm that merit aid increases enrollment in community colleges (Domina, 2014; Muñoz et al., 2016; Toutkoushian & Hillman, 2012; Zhang et al., 2013). Toutkoushian and Hillman (2012) assert that merit aid results in larger enrollment increase than state appropriations do.

With regard to other considerations that may affect greater college enrollment,

- the design of programs and how they are promoted influences college enrollment
- the more generous the program, the greater the impact
- the processes need to be made as uncomplicated as possible

NEW DIRECTIONS FOR COMMUNITY COLLEGES • DOI: 10.1002/cc

Farrell and Kienzl (2009) conclude that programs "will not magically fix all the systemic barriers to college access and in-state enrollment" (p. 170). There are many remaining questions. How many of these students would have attended a baccalaureate college had the merit aid not been available? How many of the students beginning at the community college with merit aid retain their aid and persist to degree completion? Do merit aid programs provide access to low-income students or underserved populations? These questions are especially crucial to community colleges in considering their mission to serve all students.

Community College Revenue Contexts

Decreasing state support (i.e., decreasing state appropriations offset by increasing tuition and fees) is becoming the norm in higher education. Compared with appropriation decreases experienced by 4-year institutions, community college state appropriations rose 6.4% between 1999 and 2009. However, the portion of state funding in community college operating budgets shrank from 57.1% in 1999 to 51.1% in 2009 (Romano, 2012). As enrollments increase, community colleges should seek efficiencies, remain aware of costs, and work to avoid tuition increases (D'Amico, Katsinas, & Friedel, 2012; Romano, 2012).

Rising college costs coupled with a decrease in state appropriations lead policy makers to consider additional strategies. It is no surprise that the federal government is playing a more intrusive role.

An advantage of having a national free community college program is that revenues will be more stable. However, there is concern that those who are already able to pay will receive the monies and that more students will shift to attend community colleges rather than 4-year institutions. Romano (2012) stresses that more financial aid will be necessary to offset future tuition increases; otherwise, access for those who are underserved will suffer. Community colleges must stay focused on mission and target their resources carefully.

Since broad-based merit aid implementation, practitioners, and scholars have wondered how postsecondary institutions and states themselves will respond to the addition of state merit aid programs. For example, when Georgia HOPE was implemented, tuition at 4-year institutions increased more quickly than was the case in other states' colleges and universities (Long, 2004). However, other studies reveal that this phenomenon is not widespread (Calcagno & Alfonso, 2007; Welch, 2015). Some researchers who examine what occurs at the state level claim that state investment in merit aid is not affecting other types of aid. However, other researchers assert that broad-based merit aid expands inequalities by funding those students who can already afford to attend college and plan to attend regardless of whether they receive aid, while not providing aid needed by students who come from lower socioeconomic backgrounds (Bergerson, 2009; Goldrick-

Rab, 2010; Heller & Rogers, 2006; Page & Scott-Clayton, 2016; Romano, 2005, 2012). Further research on the community college revenue contexts with respect to merit scholarships and free college programs is needed as colleges prepare to serve more students.

Practical Implications of a Nationwide Program

Resources are not growing at the same pace as enrollment. Therefore, careful planning and efficient use of available resources are crucial in responding to the students who may enter community college through a nationwide free college program. With these needs in mind, researchers point out several strategies that may help meet the needs of incoming community college students, many of whom are marginalized or underrepresented and underprepared. They include:

- partnering for transfer with local universities
- fostering community service partnerships
- offering first-year programming
- providing clear orientation and admission communication
- offering career purpose advising and planning
- assigning the best teachers to classes taken early in a student's career
- placing additional emphasis on developmental education effectiveness
- providing services for nonacademic challenges (Goldrick-Rab, 2010; Page & Scott-Clayton, 2016; Romano, 2012)

This list provides community college leaders with a starting point in considering what strategies best meet the needs of their student populations given the resources available to support implementation of the appropriate strategies.

Providing the support services necessary to help students succeed may add to institutional expenses, particularly as the number of students increase due to free college and state merit scholarships. Along with providing needed access and support, attention to quality must be maintained, which may involve extra costs to provide as well (Page & Scott-Clayton, 2016; Romano, 2012).

Student Access and Completion at Community Colleges

On the one hand, researchers point out the influence of financial aid policies, including free college and state merit scholarships, in increasing student access and completion (Conner & Rabovsky, 2011; Deming & Dynarski, 2010). On the other, researchers hold that such aid has no statistical significance when it comes to degree completion (Sjoquist & Winters, 2015; Titus, 2009). Concerns exist over providing access opportunities to more underprepared students without adding requisite services, as well as additional unforeseen consequences (Goldrick-Rab, 2010; Page & Scott-Clayton, 2016). One established consequence is that in comparison with students from middle-income families, access gaps widen for students of color and lower socioeconomic status (Page & Scott-Clayton, 2016). Learning from this, other states inserted mechanisms whereby additional supports are available to lower socioeconomic status students (Ness & Noland, 2007; Sjoquist & Winters, 2015). Researchers conjecture that free community college may affect degree completion rates by diverting students away from 4-year institutions (Romano & Palmer, 2016).

Several researchers also speak to the need to move beyond access and find ways to motivate students who participate in free college and state merit aid programs to follow through on completing college (Dynarski & Scott-Clayton, 2013; Sjoquist & Winters, 2015). Identifying additional ways to increase access and completion rates of students receiving free community college and merit scholarships are needed.

Conclusion

Paying for college continues to be a major obstacle for many students, especially for those who attend community colleges. The idea of free community college is highly symbolic, making college attendance more inviting and even conceivable to those who are not sure whether they want to attend college or believe that they may not be able to afford it. Like free community college, state merit scholarships also hold both symbolic and real value, providing dollars to students for college. However, issues relating to equitable access must be addressed.

Those working in community colleges must quickly become aware of the impact of free community college and merit scholarship programs on community college access, enrollment, and completion, as well as revenue contexts and the services that students will need to succeed. Key players need to engage in ongoing discussions that include careful examination of their community college missions. Decisions in light of what can be accomplished realistically with the resources that are available are required.

References

White House. (2015). *America's College Promise: A progress report on free community college*. Washington, DC: Author. Retrieved from https://obamawhitehouse.archives.gov/sites/default/files/docs/progressreportoncommunitycollege.pdf

Bergerson, A. A. (2009). College choice and access to college: Moving policy, research, and practice to the 21st century. [*ASHE Higher Education Report, 35*(4)]. San Francisco, CA: Jossey-Bass.

Calcagno, J. C., & Alfonso, M. (2007). *Institutional responses to state merit aid programs: The case of Florida community colleges*. New York, NY: Columbia University, Teachers College, Community College Research Center. Retrieved from https://core.ac.uk/download/files/292/27292175.pdf

Conner, T. W., & Rabovsky, T. M. (2011). Accountability, affordability, access: A review of the recent trends in higher education policy research. *Policy Studies Journal, 39*(S1), 93–112. https://doi.org/10.1111/j.1541-0072.2010.00389_7.x

Cornwell, C., Mustard, D. B., & Sridhar, D. J. (2006). The enrollment effects of merit-based financial aid: Evidence from Georgia's HOPE Program. *Journal of Labor Economics, 24*, 761–786. https://doi.org/10.1086/506485

D'Amico, M. M., Katsinas, S. G., & Friedel, J. N. (2012). The new norm: Community colleges to deal with recessionary fallout. *Community College Journal of Research and Practice, 36*, 626–631. https://doi.org/10.1080/10668926.2012.676506

Deming, D., & Dynarski, S. (2010). College aid. In P. B. Levine & D. J. Zimmerman (Eds.), *Targeting investments in children: Fighting poverty when resources are limited* (pp. 283–302). Chicago, IL: University of Chicago Press. Retrieved from http://www.nber.org/chapters/c11730

Domina T. (2014). Does merit aid program design matter? A cross-cohort analysis. *Research in Higher Education, 55*, 1–26. https://doi.org/10.1007/s11162-013-9302-y

Dynarski, S. (2004). The new merit aid. In C. Hoxby (Ed.), *College choices: The economics of where to go, when to go, and how to pay for it* (pp. 63–100). Chicago, IL: University of Chicago Press. Retrieved from http://www.nber.org/chapters/c10098.pdf

Dynarski, S., & Scott-Clayton, J. (2013). Financial aid policy: Lessons from research. *Future of Children, 23*, 67–91. Retrieved from http://files.eric.ed.gov/fulltext/EJ1015227.pdf

Farrell, P. L., & Kienzl, G. S. (2009). Are state non-need, merit-based scholarship programs impacting college enrollment? *Education Finance and Policy, 4*, 150–174. https://doi.org/10.1162/edfp.2009.4.2.150

Field, K. (2015, January 20). Six years in, six years to go, only modest progress on Obama's college-completion goal. *Chronicle of Higher Education,* A6. Retrieved from http://www.chronicle.com/article/6-Years-in6-to-Go-Only/151303

Goldrick-Rab, S. (2010). Challenges and opportunities for improving community college student success. *Review of Educational Research, 80*, 437–469. Retrieved from http://www.jstor.org/stable/40927288

Heller, D. E., & Rogers, K. R. (2006). Shifting the burden: Public and private financing of higher education in the United States and implications for Europe. *Tertiary Education and Management, 12*, 91–117. https://doi.org/10.1007/s11233-006-0001-5

Ingle, W. K., & Ratliff, J. R. (2015). Then and now: An analysis of broad-based merit aid initial eligibility policies after twenty years. *Kentucky Journal of Higher Education Policy and Practice, 3*(2), Article 3. Retrieved from http://uknowledge.uky.edu/kjhepp/vol3/iss2/3

Long, B. T. (2004). How do financial aid policies affect colleges? The institutional impact of the Georgia HOPE Scholarship. *Journal of Human Resources, 39*, 1045–1066.

Looney, A., & Yannelis, C. (2015). *A crisis in student loans? How changes in the characteristics of borrowers and in the institutions they attend contributed to the rising loan defaults* (Brookings Papers on Economic Activity). BPEA Conference Draft. Washington, DC: Brookings Institution. Retrieved from http://www.brookings.edu/yabout/projects/bpea/papers/2015/looney-yannelis-student-loan-defaults

Muñoz, J., Harrington, J., Curs, B. R., & Ehlert, M. (2016). Democratization and diversion: The effect of Missouri's A+ Schools Program on postsecondary enrollment. *Journal of Higher Education, 87*(6), 801–830. Retrieved from https://www.researchgate.net/profile/Bradley_Curs/publication/267392540_Democratization_and_Diversion_The_Effect_of_Missouri's_A_Schools_Program_on_Postsecondary_Enrollment/links/55843d6608aeb0cdaddbb474.pdf

National Conference of State Legislatures. (2016, April 25). *Free community colleges.* Retrieved from http://www.ncsl.org/research/education/free-community-college.aspx

Ness, E. C. (2008). *Merit aid and the politics of education.* New York, NY: Routledge.

Ness, E. C., & Noland, B. E. (2007). Targeted merit aid: Implications of the Tennessee Education Lottery Scholarship Program. *Journal of Student Financial Aid, 37,* 7–17. Retrieved from http://publications.nasfaa.org/jsfa/vol37/iss1/4

Page, L. C., & Scott-Clayton, J. (2016). Improving college access in the United States: Barriers and policy responses. *Economics of Education Review, 51,* 4–22. https://doi.org/10.1016/j.econedurev.2016.02.009

Romano, R. M. (2005). Seeking the proper balance between tuition, state support, and local revenues: An economic perspective. In S. G. Katsinas & J. C. Palmer (Eds.), *New Directions for Community Colleges: No. 132. Sustaining financial support for community colleges* (pp. 33–41). San Francisco, CA: Jossey-Bass. https://doi.org/10.1002/cc.213

Romano, R. M. (2012). Looking behind community college budgets for future policy considerations. *Community College Review, 40,* 165–189. https://doi.org/10.1177/0091552112441824

Romano, R. M., & Palmer, J. C. (2016). *Financing community colleges: Where we are, where we're going.* New York, NY: Rowman & Littlefield.

Sjoquist, D. L., & Winters, J. V. (2015). State merit-based financial aid programs and college attainment. *Journal of Regional Science, 55,* 364–390. doi: https://10:1111/jors.12161

Titus, M. A. (2009). The production of bachelor's degrees and financial aspects of state higher education policy: A dynamic analysis. *Journal of Higher Education, 80,* 439–468. https://doi.org/10.1353/jhe.0.0055

Toutkoushian, R. K., & Hillman, N. W. (2012). The impact of state appropriations and grants on access to higher education and outmigration. *Review of Higher Education, 51,* 51–90. https://doi.org/10.1353/rhe.2012.0063

Welch, J. G. (2015). *Three essays on the economics of higher education: How students and colleges respond to financial aid programs* (Doctoral dissertation). Knoxville: University of Tennessee. Retrieved from http://trace.tennessee.edu/utk_graddiss/3481

Zhang, L., Hu, S., & Sensenig, V. (2013). The effect of Florida's Bright Futures Program on college enrollment and degree production: An aggregated-level analysis. *Research in Higher Education, 54,* 746–764. https://doi.org/10.1007/s11162-013-9293-8

LORI ELLIOTT BUCHANAN *is a professor in the department of Library Administration at Austin Peay State University and a doctoral student at Western Kentucky University.*

KRISTIN BAILEY WILSON *is an associate professor in the department of Educational Administration, Leadership, and Research at Western Kentucky University.*

8

This chapter addresses how dual enrollment programs support the community college mission, specifically related to access and completion.

Supporting the Mission Through Dual Enrollment

Stephanie J. Jones

Community college missions unify a college's efforts toward a singular focus, which prevents competing missions from gaining momentum (Velcoff & Ferrari, 2006). These missions are complex, multifaceted, comprehensive—and some would say—impossible to fulfill. The focus of this chapter is to examine how dual enrollment contributes to the mission of community colleges. For the purposes of this discussion, dual enrollment is defined as college courses taken by high school students, regardless of whether they are receiving both high school and college credit for the same course. Because of the variations in state policies relative to dual enrollment, the state of Texas is main focus in this discussion.

Dual Enrollment as Part of Mission

Many initiatives to increase access to higher education have shown success over the past decades, but access is only one piece of the puzzle; getting in the door is important—but leaving with a credential is even more so. Higher education institutions are being challenged through many national initiatives such as the American Graduation Initiative not only to admit students but to ensure they complete—often referred to as the completion agenda through policy and research literature (Evenbeck & Johnson, 2012; McPhail, 2011). Those who are proponents of community colleges identify them as the institutions that are the most nimble, dynamic, and responsive to change and can meet training and workforce challenges much quicker than their 4-year counterparts. These institutions have the capabilities to successfully produce a large number of educated individuals to supply a qualified workforce to ensure a successful U.S. economy (White House, 2009).

New Directions for Community Colleges, no. 180, Winter 2017 © 2017 Wiley Periodicals, Inc.
Published online in Wiley Online Library (wileyonlinelibrary.com) • DOI: 10.1002/cc.20283

The Alliance for Excellent Education (2010) reports that 60% of jobs require some form of higher education and 90% of the fastest-growing, high-wage jobs in the United States require a credential. The national high school graduation rate is at an all-time high, but one in five high school students fail to earn a high school diploma on time. In addition, the failure of rural students to pursue education past high school is a growing and pervasive problem. The Alliance for Excellent Education also claims that "when one out of every four students fails to graduate from our rural high schools; it's not just a 'local' issue: it's a national crisis" (p. 1). Approximately 25% of rural students fail to graduate from high school, and the failure rates are even higher for students of color. Within rural communities, only 17% of adults age 25 and over have completed college. This is half the college completion rate of their peers in urban areas. In rural America, the quality and performance of local high schools have a direct impact on their communities' abilities to attract new industries and achieve economic growth. Therefore, the need to increase high school graduation rates and college matriculation is essential for all communities but may be more so for rural communities to survive. Access to programs that enable students to participate in and earn college credit while in high school, often at free or lower tuition rates, can help to alleviate some of the financial stresses of higher education (Cassidy, Keating, & Young, 2010; Jones, 2014; Karp & Hughes, 2008).

State Policy and Dual Enrollment

States are able to meet reform goals pertinent to increasing higher education participation rates as well as college completion through the involvement of community colleges in dual enrollment initiatives (Welsh, Brake, & Choi, 2005). Educators and policy makers continue to examine policies and practices to find ways to encourage students to matriculate to college. Within states that have large dual enrollment programming, many are likely to establish regulations, as enrollment numbers and resulting revenues generated from dual enrollment may encourage 2-year colleges to lobby for legislation that protects their interests (Mokher & McLendon, 2009).

In a study of the 2010–2011 academic year conducted by Marken, Gray, and Lewis (2013), 98% of 490 public 2-year colleges that responded to their survey across the United States had high school students enrolled in college courses, with 96% of them enrolled through dual enrollment programs. Findings of this study were that these institutions enrolled 980,000 of the 1,363,500 high school students nationwide enrolled in college courses. In most states, community colleges are the main providers of dual enrollment opportunities (Hoffman, Vargas, & Santos, 2009), but this could be changing in some states such as Texas, because of legislative changes.

The Education Commission of the States ([ESC], 2015) compiled an extensive profile of dual enrollment programs in all states, as well as the eligibility requirements mandated in state policies. This analysis identified eligibility policies related to grade level, grade point average (GPA), written approval/recommendation for participation, and entrance requirements of higher education institutions. In 22 states, students had to be in their junior year in high school to participate in dual enrollment, whereas in several states, students could enroll in their sophomore year. Minimum high school GPA standards were required in 7 states, written approval and/or a recommendation from a high school or higher education official was required in 22 states, and 25 states had course prerequisites or placement standards. Many states also had other eligibility criteria, such as scores on state-approved secondary or postsecondary examinations, completion of prescribed high school courses, or permission from parents. Within 11 states, the local secondary schools or higher education institutions were allowed to determine eligibility standards, and in 14 states, the eligibility requirements varied based on the type of dual enrollment coursework or program a student was pursuing.

A large number of state dual enrollment policies focus on providing opportunities for high-achieving students, as evidenced by the fact that many states require students to demonstrate eligibility through high school GPA or performance on college readiness tests (An, 2013; Barnett & Stamm, 2010). These requirements may hinder participation in dual enrollment courses (An, 2013; Karp, Bailey, Hughes, & Fermin, 2004). Consequently, there is a national trend occurring of providing greater access to dual enrollment programs for "disadvantaged, first-generation, and middle-achieving students" (Community College Research Center, 2012, p. 1).

According to Hoffman et al. (2009), "most dual-enrollment programs offer free or discounted tuition, providing some savings for families who otherwise might not afford to send their children to college" (p. 45). However, reduced or waived tuition may cause problems for institutions, as colleges who bear the cost of dual enrollment coursework may be unable to expand their programs due to financial constraints (Meyer, 2004), as someone must pay or institutions must relinquish revenues (Karp et al., 2004). This is especially concerning as community colleges continue to see downward trends in state allocations, resulting in a greater percentage of operating budgets coming from tuition and fees (Romano, 2012).

Dual enrollment opportunities for high school students have flourished as the movement to enable more students to complete college has gained momentum (Mangan, 2014). As a result, dual enrollment has grown to become an important component of public higher education in Texas and, in particular, at community colleges. In 2006, the Texas legislature passed House Bill 1 (HB1), which mandates that high schools provide more access to pathways to earn college credit while in high school (Texas Education Agency, 2006). HB1 provides funding opportunities for dual enrollment participation and was designed to increase college readiness rates by the state by granting a $275 per student allotment for high schools to support individual achievement of college-ready standards. K–12 superintendents and college presidents have had the opportunity to leverage these funds to provide accelerated academic catch up strategies and supports that help underrepresented students graduate college ready, including by completing college courses in high school. Unfortunately, not all school districts have used HB1 funding to support this initiative.

Since HB1 implementation in the 2008–2009 academic year, according to the Texas Higher Education Coordinating Board ([THECB], n.d.), enrollments in dual enrollment courses grew by about 15,000 students between Fall 2007 and Fall 2008, and 12,000 students between Fall 2008 and Fall 2009. By Fall 2012, 99,452 high school students were enrolled in dual enrollment courses, with 95,774 of these students enrolled at public community and technical colleges. Dual enrollment students comprised 6.8% of the students enrolled in Texas postsecondary institutions in Fall 2012 (THECB, n.d.). According to statistics released by the THECB (2011) for the period of Fall 2000 to Fall 2010, participation in dual enrollment of White students grew by 320%, African American students by 965%, Hispanic students by 951%, and those identified as Asian or other ethnic groups grew by 1,254%.

In 2015–2016, the state of Texas through HB 505 changed the policy regulations for dual enrollment. These changes included that there is no limit on the number of college credit courses or hours that a high school student may enroll in (each semester and academic year), and there is no limit on the grade level at which a high school student can be eligible to enroll in dual enrollment courses (Lofters, 2015). Another recent change is covered in section 130.008 of the Texas education code, which states that school districts no longer are confined or obligated to receive dual enrollment offerings from the community college that serves their service area (Texas Education Code, n.d.). School districts in Texas can select the provider of their choice for dual enrollment courses, with limitations on the number of courses they can take from that provider. These policies have direct impact on community colleges in Texas being the main contributor of dual enrollment courses within the state.

Effectiveness of Dual Enrollment Programs

As noted previously, dual enrollment enables high students to receive both high school and college credit for the same coursework, while exposing students to a more challenging curricula, and offers a wealth of other noted benefits. Among these benefits, dual enrollment participation encourages students to pursue a college degree, addresses "senioritis"—making better use of the high school senior year, and exposes students to the experience of attending college in a safe environment (An, 2013; Barnett & Stamm, 2010; Jones, 2014; Karp, 2012; Struhl & Vargas, 2012). Dual enrollment is a way to encourage high school students who are at risk to pursue postsecondary education (Barnett & Stamm, 2010; Cassidy et al., 2010; Hofmann, 2012) and is seen as a mechanism to reduce the time it takes to earn a college

New Directions for Community Colleges • DOI: 10.1002/cc

degree and reduce the costs of a college education, as many colleges reduce or waive the tuition for dual enrollment courses (Barnett & Stamm, 2010; Cassidy et al., 2010; Jones, 2014; Karp & Hughes, 2008).

In its various forms, dual enrollment is associated with potentially improved coherence between high school and college curricula, increased access to college, reduced need for remedial coursework, improved quality of technical training for workers, easier recruitment of students to college, and reduced college expenses (Bailey, Hughes, & Karp, 2003). The research verifying these benefits is limited, though. Citing research from the Community College Research Center's 2007 study on dual enrollment, Vargas (2010) reports that when compared to nondual enrollment participants, students who participate in dual enrollment have higher college enrollment and persistence rates through the second year of college and higher college GPAs through the second year. The research also shows that these benefits appear to be greatest for students typically underrepresented in college, but the schools with the highest minority enrollments are the least likely to offer dual enrollment courses.

A large body of literature is available on dual enrollment and much of it outlines the many benefits to students specifically, who participate in dual enrollment coursework while in high school. Several studies find that participation in dual enrollment has a positive impact on GPA and student persistence rates once students matriculate to college after high school graduation (An, 2013; CCRC, 2012; Jones, 2014; Kretchmar & Farmer, 2013; Young, 2013). The higher persistence rates are seen during the first to second semester in college (a time when most students stop out), and from the first to second year in college, in addition to better degree attainment are seen (CCRC, 2012; D'Amico, Morgan, Robertson, & Rivers, 2013; Jones, 2014; Struhl & Vargas, 2012; THECB, n.d., 2011).

In addition to the benefits that correlate with dual enrollment, there are some criticisms. In addition to what has been mentioned previously about these programs being focused mainly on high-achieving students, resulting in limited opportunities for those at the middle or lower levels of academic achievement, there is also a concern with high school students being unsuccessful in their dual enrollment courses, resulting in the transcription of poor grades on a college transcript prior to graduating from high school (Bradley, 2013; Karp & Hughes, 2008; Jones, 2014). If a dual enrollment course is taken concurrently for both high school and college credit, failure of the course could affect the high school requirements for graduation. In addition to the academic ramifications for high school students, the literature and critics address the quality of courses taught on high school campuses and whether these courses actually benefit high school students with their college transition (Evenbeck & Johnson, 2012; Karp & Hughes, 2008; Texas State Auditor's Office, 2010). Karp et al. (2004) and Jones (2014) claim that some courses taught on a high school campus may not meet the expectations of a rigorous college-level course taught on the college campus. Another concern cited in the literature had to do with the increased emphasis on pushing students to complete college quickly in order to increase completion rates and time to degree, which may affect the knowledge transition that is supposed to occur in high school and college (Evenbeck & Johnson, 2012; Mangan, 2014; Tinberg & Nadeau, 2013).

Conclusion

One of the most important missions of the community college is to provide access to postsecondary education for all people but especially to those populations who are underrepresented. It would be difficult to claim that dual enrollment programs offered by community colleges are not helping these institutions to meet their mission. High school students, specifically those in rural locations, who enroll and successfully complete dual enrollment courses are more likely to enter postsecondary education and are more likely to complete their higher education goal. Not only does the research support this is for all dual enrollment students but more specifically for underrepresented student populations. Dual enrollment has been shown to accelerate time to degree attainment, decrease the costs of a higher education, as well as help states and the nation meet their goals for an educated workforce.

Based on the discussion of dual enrollment, the following recommendations are offered to community colleges to ensure their dual enrollment offerings do support their mission. The first recommendation is that community colleges and secondary schools must move past their focus on high-achieving high school students and implement programs and services to help prepare underserved student populations, as well. There is significant evidence that supports this exposure is instrumental to their future success.

The second recommendation is focused on college administrators and community college faculty. Dual enrollment students must be exposed to the best faculty the college offers. Highly qualified college faculty will have the most impact on high school students by introducing them to the rigors of college and outlining the expectations in their first college-level experiences. Failure as a college to perceive or recognize the importance of this exposure and engagement will continue to breed the criticisms of dual enrollment as nonrigorous college credit, leading to many colleges and universities continuing to not accept credits for transfer.

In order to increase the number of students in higher education, policy makers, college, and school district administrators must recognize that not everyone understands the higher education system. Of specific concern for all involved is how to provide programs and services to underserved students and their parents so that they understand what it means to go to college and what it takes to be successful. Through their mission, community colleges have a responsibility to serve all students and ensure their access and success.

References

Alliance for Excellent Education. (2010). *Current challenges and opportunities in preparing rural high school student for success in college and careers: What federal policymakers need to know.* Washington, DC: Author.

An, B. P. (2013). The influence of dual enrollment on academic performance and college readiness: Differences by socioeconomic status. *Research in Higher Education, 54,* 407–432. https://doi.org/10.1007/s11162-012-0278-z

Bailey, T. R., Hughes, K. L., & Karp, M. M. (2003). *Dual enrollment programs: Easing transitions from high school to college* (CCRC Brief, 17). New York, NY: Columbia University, Teachers College, Community College Research Center. Retrieved from https://academiccommons.columbia.edu/catalog/ac:157417

Barnett, E., & Stamm, L. (2010). *Dual enrollment: A strategy for educational advancement of all students.* Washington, DC: Blackboard Institute.

Bradley, P. (2013, March 18). Doubling down: Florida colleges struggle to fund fast-growing dual enrollment programs. *Community College Week,* 6–7.

Cassidy, L., Keating, K., & Young, V. (2010). *Dual enrollment: Lessons learned on school-level implementation.* Retrieved from http://www2.ed.gov/programs/slcp/finaldual.pdf

Community College Research Center. (2012). *What we know about dual enrollment.* New York: Columbia University, Teachers College, Community College Research Center. Retrieved from http://ccrc.tc.columbia.edu/publications/what-we-know-about-dual-enrollment.html

D'Amico, M. M., Morgan, G. B., Robertson, S., & Rivers, H. E. (2013). Dual enrollment variables and college student persistence. *Community College Journal of Research and Practice, 37*(10), 769–779. https://doi.org/10.1080/10668921003723334

Education Commission of the States. (2015). Individual state profile: Dual enrollment – all state profiles. Retrieved from http://ecs.force.com/mbdata/mbprofallRT?Rep=DE14A

Evenbeck, S., & Johnson, K. E. (2012). Students must not become victims of the completion agenda. *Liberal Education, 98*(1), 26–33.

Hofmann, E. (2012). Why dual enrollment? In E. Hofmann & D. Voloch (Eds.), *New Directions for Higher Education: No. 158. Dual enrollment: Strategies, outcomes, and lessons for school–college partnerships* (pp. 1–8). San Francisco, CA: Jossey-Bass. https://doi.org/10.1002/he.20009

Hoffman, N., Vargas, J., & Santos, J. (2009). New directions for dual enrollment: Creating stronger pathways from high school through college. In A. C. Bueschel & A. Venezia (Eds.), *New Directions for Community Colleges: No. 145. Policies and practices to improve student preparation and success* (pp. 43–58). San Francisco, CA: Jossey-Bass. https://doi.org/10.1002/cc.354

Jones, S. J. (2014). Student participation in dual enrollment and college success. *Community College Journal of Research and Practice, 38*(1), 24–37. https://doi.org/10.1080/10668926.2010.532449

Karp, M. M. (2012). "I don't know, I've never been to college!": Dual enrollment as a college readiness strategy. In E. Hofmann & D. Voloch (Eds.), *New Directions for Higher Education: No. 158. Dual enrollment: Strategies, outcomes, and lessons for school–college partnerships* (pp. 39–47). San Francisco, CA: Jossey-Bass. https://doi:10.1002/he.20011

Karp, M. M., Bailey, T. R., Hughes, K. L., & Fermin, B. J. (2004). *State dual enrollment policies: Addressing access and quality.* Washington, DC: U.S. Department of Education.

Karp, M. M., & Hughes, K. L. (2008, October). Study: Dual enrollment can benefit a broad range of students. *Techniques, 83*(7), 14–17.

Kretchmar, J., & Farmer, S. (2013). How much is enough? Rethinking the role of high school courses in college admission. *Journal of College Admission, 220,* 28–33.

Lofters, A. (2015). *Dual credit legislative updated*. Austin, TX: Texas Higher Education Coordinating Board. Retrieved from http://www.thecb.state.tx.us/reports/PDF/6975.PDF?CFID=46929531&CFTOKEN=52815953

Mangan, K. (2014, February 17). Is faster always better? *Chronicle of Higher Education*. Retrieved from http://www.chronicle.com/article/Is-Faster-Always-Better-/144781

Marken, S., Gray, L., & Lewis, L. (2013). *Dual enrollment programs and courses for high school students at postsecondary institutions: 2010–11* (NCES 2013-002). Washington, DC: U.S. Department of Education, National Center for Education Statistics.

McPhail, C. J. (2011). *The completion agenda: A call to action. Summary report from the November 10–11, 2010, meeting of the American Association of Community Colleges Commissions and Board of Directors*. Washington, DC: American Association of Community Colleges. Retrieved from http://www.aacc.nche.edu/Publications/Reports/Documents/CompletionAgenda_report.pdf

Meyer, H. (2004, October 25). Report examines dual enrollment, suggests reforms. *Community College Week, 17*(6), 2–10.

Mokher, C. G., & McLendon, M. K. (2009). Uniting secondary and postsecondary education: An event history analysis of state adoption of dual enrollment policies. *American Journal of Education, 115,* 249–277.

Romano, R. M. (2012). Looking behind community college budgets for future policy considerations. *Community College Review, 40*(2), 165–189. https://doi.org/10.1177/0091552112441824

Struhl, B., & Vargas, J. (2012). *Taking college courses in high school: A strategy for college readiness*. Boston, MA: Jobs for the Future.

Texas Education Agency. (2006). *Briefing book on House Bill 1 79th Texas legislature, 3rd called session*. Austin, TX: Author.

Texas Education Code. (n.d.). Chapter 130, Junior College Districts. Retrieved from http://www.statutes.legis.state.tx.us/Docs/ED/htm/ED.130.htm

Texas Higher Education Coordinating Board. (n.d.). *Dual credit data*. Retrieved from http://www.txhighereddata.org/Interactive/HSCollLink2.CFM

Texas Higher Education Coordinating Board. (2011). *Dual credit report: In satisfaction of Rider 33 of the Appropriations Act*. Austin, TX: Author.

Texas State Auditor's Office. (2010). *An audit report on dual credit programs at selected public school districts and higher education institutions* (Report No. 11–0026). Austin, TX: Author. Retrieved from http://www.sao.state.tx.us/reports/main/11-006.pdf

Tinberg, H., & Nadeau, J. (2013). What happens when high school students write in a college course: A study of dual credit. *English Journal, 102*(5), 35–42.

Vargas, J. (2010). *Dual enrollment in Texas: State polices that strengthens new pathways to and through college for low-income youth*. Transcript of testimony before the Texas State Senate: Joint Interim Hearing of Senate Higher Education Committee and Senate Education Committee on dual enrollment on May 24, 2010.

Velcoff, J., & Ferrari, J. R. (2006). Perceptions of university mission by senior administrators: Relating to faculty engagement. *Christian Higher Education, 5*(4), 329–339. https://doi.org/10.1080/15363750500408090

Welsh, J. F., Brake, N., & Choi, N. (2005). Student participation and performance in dual-credit courses in a reform environment. *Community College Journal of Research and Practice, 29*(3), 199–203. https://doi.org/10.1080/10668920590901158

White House. (2009). *Remarks by the President on the American Graduation Initiative in Warren, MI*. Retrieved from https://obamawhitehouse.archives.gov/the-press-office/remarks-president-american-graduation-initiative-warren-mi

Young, R. D. (2013). *Dual credit enrollment and GPA by ethnicity and gender at Texas 2-year colleges* (Doctoral dissertation). Retrieved from ProQuest. (3571399)

DR. STEPHANIE J. JONES *is an associate professor in higher education and asso-ciate department chairperson of Educational Psychology & Leadership at Texas Tech University.*

NEW DIRECTIONS FOR COMMUNITY COLLEGES • DOI: 10.1002/cc

9

This chapter advises community college leaders how to achieve mission balance by using strategic planning to make mission-critical decisions and take decisive action.

Meeting the Challenges of Expanding Missions Through Strategic Planning

David M. Hellmich, Greg J. Feeney

Defining critical missions has been an ongoing process at most community colleges for approximately 50 years. Over time, with one budget crisis followed by another and another, with one external mandate followed by another and another, most of these colleges have settled into defined, usually revered, missions. Yes, colleges periodically revise their mission statements, mostly to avoid trouble with the regional accrediting agency. Do the revised mission statements alter the critical missions of the college? Almost never. Yes, colleges create and periodically revise strategic plans, again, mostly to appease the regional accrediting agency and because "it is what forward-thinking organizations do." Are these strategic plans strategic? Typically not.

In practice, community college leaders have moved their considerations from defining critical missions to the pragmatics of how to balance these missions with ever-fewer resources and ever-greater external demands. Institutional success—and the corresponding success of senior leadership—depends on balancing critical missions and evolving the college culture so students, staff, faculty, trustees, alumni, and the community citizenry understand and embrace this balance.

How leaders achieve critical mission balance and how they evolve college culture are questions best answered within the context of the institution's strategic planning process. Strategic planning too often begins and ends with operational planning. Although important, operational planning is not strategic planning. The goal of operational planning is to improve current operations, for example, changing to a new learning management system to meet faculty and student online needs. The goal of strategic planning is to realign institutional resources, in particular human resources, in a calculated manner to change the college, for example, adding personnel

NEW DIRECTIONS FOR COMMUNITY COLLEGES, no. 180, Winter 2017 © 2017 Wiley Periodicals, Inc.
Published online in Wiley Online Library (wileyonlinelibrary.com) • DOI: 10.1002/cc.20284

to the college's foundation to develop alternative revenue sources. A completed strategic plan is not strategic if it has a myriad of goals and objectives connected to all of the functional areas of the college. If leaders are to be successful in the ongoing balancing of critical missions and evolving of the college culture, they must implement effective strategic planning.

Even when committed to changing their institutions, leaders must overcome the three plagues of strategic planning: the deeply rooted cultural expectation that strategic planning will be much ado about very little; the pervasive fear that if, by chance, there is meaningful change as a result of strategic planning, this change will conflict with entrenched institutional values; and the institutional inertia that will fight change long after the need for and the path to change have been decided. We offer the following four points of emphasis, born from our combined 45 years of experience at five community colleges in four states, to assist leaders as they attempt to implement successful strategic planning: identifying key institutional players and getting their support, giving voice to these key players as well as internal and external constituents, reflecting on core institutional values when making the critical mission-balancing decisions, and acting decisively after critical mission balance has been determined.

We anchor our points of emphasis with McPhail and McPhail's strategic planning framework (2006). Many frameworks exist, and our points of emphasis can find a home in most planning frameworks. We use McPhail and McPhail because they describe a thoughtful, step-by-step process. McPhail and McPhail begin with scoping out current mission priorities, followed by clarifying the focus and importance of each mission, establishing broad expectations, establishing evidence-based assessment criteria and mission priorities, and developing an implementation and results management plan. The authors use Cohen and Brawer's fivefold description of community college missions (student services, career education, developmental education, community education, and the collegiate function) and assert that by using their framework, a college will land on its prioritized mission or missions. In so doing, "some colleges may choose to support one high-quality mission; others may sustain four or five missions" (McPhail & McPhail, 2006, p. 98).

We take some exception to McPhail and McPhail. Not only do we see the student services mission as being foundational to all other missions and irrelevant without one or more of these other missions (thus, a college never would choose to support only one high-quality mission), but also we contend that if a college were to choose to support fewer missions, it likely would have had to make this choice during previous financial crises. More to the point, leaders are struggling with how to balance existing missions; they are struggling with how to preserve these missions while keeping the doors open.

Our first two points of emphasis (identifying key institutional players and getting their support and giving voice to these key players as well as internal and external constituents) should be considered before embarking on strategic planning. Without the support of key players, strategic planning is the waste of time everyone expects it to be. Our next point of emphasis (reflecting on core institutional values driving the critical mission-balancing decisions) should be considered when establishing evidence-based mission priorities. Finally, leaders must act decisively while developing the implementation and results management plan.

Identifying Functional Leaders and Getting Their Support

Before launching the latest strategic plan, leaders must identify the institution's functional leaders and get their support. In practice, functional leaders are the influential players in the work of the college. They are the ring leaders and the in-the-know personnel who may be found in any structural role. Whether they hold formal leadership positions is unimportant. Functional leaders are influential in a more powerful way—by practice. Accordingly, three pragmatic ways leaders can identify functional leaders are by considering interpersonal communication skills, listening skills, and informal organizational structures.

Interpersonal communication expertise is a significant trait of most functional leaders. Their ability to use interpersonal skills to build and maintain strong relationships strengthens information flow and leads to greater college success. Designated authority and/or titles work only to the extent of the person's skill set, which is often illustrated when colleges have multiple people at a particular level, for example, vice president and dean. Although two colleagues have a similar title and rank, the differences in their level of influence are often reflective of their competence in interpersonal communication. Leaders with relationship skills are typically more influential; they show themselves to be key players in the life of the college.

In discussing the second variable in identifying functional leaders, we narrow our communication focus to listening. Essentially, listening is about assigning meaning. Skilled listening provides the opportunity to gain insight not only into an individual's perspective but also into the greater social tone related to an issue and the organization. The better the understanding of the breadth and depth of this process, the better the ability to assess how individuals respond to both topics and others, thus strengthening the ability to recognize key players in the context of the topic.

Good listeners often emerge as functional leaders because individuals gravitate toward them. Functional leaders listen and act inclusively. They care about the perspectives of others, and their focus and decisions are information based. Listening in our modern environment encompasses everything from face-to-face interactions to social media. It is an active and intentional process. The strength of this process is exemplified by Llopis (2013):

NEW DIRECTIONS FOR COMMUNITY COLLEGES • DOI: 10.1002/cc

As a leader, it's difficult to really know what your employees are thinking about, what's troubling them or how to help them get out of a performance slump—unless you take the time to listen to them. Listening goes well beyond being quiet and giving someone your full attention. It requires you to be aware of body language, facial expressions, mood, and natural behavioral tendencies. Listening should be a full-time job when you consider the uncertainty embedded in the workplace and the on-going changes taking place. (p. 2)

Llopis recognizes the contextual nature of listening. The impact builds on itself: effective listening creates a positive work climate by increasing the understanding of individual and organizational ideas and challenges. This, in turn, increases communication from individuals to organizational leaders. Functional leaders are naturally revealed through this process of active listening.

The third component of identifying functional leadership is giving attention to both formal and informal organizational structures. Institutional activities are shaped by both structures. Formal structures are defined and publicized by the college; the understanding of informal structures is more nuanced and dependent on the general relationships within the college and community. This understanding builds on the interpersonal and listening communication variables because informal structures are generally based on camaraderie. Further, the stronger a person's relationships with those in the college, the better is his or her understanding of the informal structures. As these structures are often viewed as gossip channels, a waste of time or distractions, informal structures make some nervous. Lunenburg (2010) stated, "Although leaders may be reluctant to use the grapevine, they should always listen to it. The grapevine is a natural phenomenon that serves as a means of emotional release for staff members and provides the administrator with significant information concerning the attitudes and feelings of staff members" (p. 5). The significance of informal channels is contingent on a leader's savvy in understanding and using them. Further, functional leaders are often at the center of these structures. The better a leader's understanding of the informal organizational structures within a college, the better that person's ability to identify functional leaders, as they are often one and the same. This understanding requires keen insight into the pragmatic communication flow rather than focusing solely on the formal structure.

When learning about the development of a new strategic plan, the college community first will look to see if its functional leaders are connected to the plan's development. Leaders will be able to identify these functional leaders through examining interpersonal communication skills, listening skills, and formal and informal organizational structures and will be able to reach out to them for their involvement. Next, the college community will ask its functional leaders if this process is worth its time. The answer to that question is contingent upon the functional leaders perceiving they and others will have meaningful voices in the strategic plan.

Giving Voice

Giving voice to functional leaders and internal and external constituents relates to more than asking for input. Leaders must recognize the complexity in giving others voice. The more they understand this complexity, the more they can create a culture where others are willing to share information and some are eager to take the lead in initiating information sharing.

A lesson for individuals when they step into leadership is the realization that perceived power often leads to others pandering and playing the game to politic and to stay in good graces. Some leaders may think they are different from others, that those they work with see them more as a colleague than a boss. The reality is others often see a title more than the individual. To battle this reality, a leader must steadily work to create a reputation as someone who values all perspectives. Although this can be a challenge, the foundation is others having voice. The stronger this foundation the more likely leaders are to receive valuable information from both visible functional leaders and those yet to be revealed. Three foundational steps to giving others voice are asking authentic questions, being mindful of one's own perspective, and being mindful of others' agendas.

Authentic questions reinforce a culture of inclusion where individuals feel valued; this culture is demonstrated in practice more than words. Authentic questions seek other perspectives and incorporate those perspectives within decision making. Thus, what makes questions authentic relies more on what is done with the answers than on the questions themselves. The antithesis is counterfeit questions that, intentional or not, are asked to create the illusion of inclusion. This ruse may lead to perceived short-term efficiencies, but the practice creates a negative environment that weakens voice. The perception that a question is counterfeit may have nothing to do with what was asked but with the perception that previous feedback was ignored. Leaders demonstrate authenticity by how they identify the inclusiveness of input, which does not mean vocal people always get what they want. It distinctly means leaders validate the ultimate decision in the context of feedback. Doing so makes it less likely for others to perceive their input was ignored. Effective leaders articulate the input process and make transparent how competing perspectives are evaluated. Authentic questions are the foundation of giving voice.

Another important aspect to giving voice is leaders having awareness of their own goals and biases and their ability to manage them. Inclusive leaders are mindful of personal motivations and transparent in relation to their own goals. They set aside their answers and focus on understanding others' perspectives. Like effective listening, this is an active and intentional process. Simple questions that illustrate whether a leader is focusing on understanding others' perspectives include the following: How strongly does the leader have a result in mind? How open is the leader to other conclusions? Is the leader willing to support the success of other conclusions? Answers to these questions indicate whether a leader is prepared to ask authentic questions.

Colleagues can produce a commonly overlooked challenge to creating a culture of inclusion. Thus, leaders must be mindful of how others' agendas might impede voice. A common challenge is others working to limit discussion. The classic example is someone so focused on getting agreement or disagreement the person works to get to his or her desired result with minimal discussion. The complexity of providing voice is further demonstrated when others are not as motivated by the college's success as they are by their individual achievement. A typical example is someone being so focused on defining a pet project as successful that contradicting data and messages are ignored. The damage of such situations goes beyond the particular project to the downward spiral of challenging voice and damaging organizational climate.

Asking authentic questions, being mindful of one's own biases, and being mindful of others' agendas strengthen voice. These foundational tools help create a culture that promotes active and ongoing dialogue. Such a culture is a prerequisite to beginning strategic planning.

Reflecting on Core Institutional Values

Now that the institution's functional leaders have been identified and support the strategic planning process because they are convinced their own and others' voices will contribute to shaping the process, we move to the point in McPhail and McPhail's framework when critical mission-balancing decisions are made. It is here the strategic part of strategic planning becomes problematic. It is here even the most committed college and community members may fear that considered changes will conflict with their deep-seated views of what is most valued at the college. An approach for mollifying this fear is to reflect openly on core institutional values when making the critical mission-balancing decisions. Turning to the ethics of critique and local community can assist with this reflection.

Wood and Hilton (2012) discuss the ethics of critique and local community as two of five ethical paradigms for community college leaders. The ethic of critique "is a morally based paradigm . . . . employed by individuals who strive to create parity for others who have been disadvantaged by society" (p. 202). The ethic of local community "situates the best interests of the local community as a cardinal principle in decision making" (p. 206). Considering these ethics at that supremely important moment in the strategic planning process when evidence-based mission priorities are established reminds everyone of the core community college values of providing access to those most in need of access and meeting community social, cultural, and economic needs.

Applying these ethics is illustrated in the following scenario when two programs, one within the developmental education mission and the other within the career education mission, are considered for elimination.

The college's leadership team has to cut $750,000 from next fiscal year's $20 million budget. Team members have thoughtfully gone through steps 1–4 of McPhail and McPhail's framework: they have scoped out current mission priorities, they have clarified the focus and importance of each mission, they have established broad expectations, and they have established evidence-based assessment criteria.

First, do they cut the adult education program, which importantly is placed within the developmental education mission, not the community education mission, because adult education curricula anchor the low end of the math, reading, English continuum? Adult education is at the top of the list of possible programs to cut, partly because it is funded separately by state and federal dollars, which in this scenario the college likely will not get, resulting in the deficit increasing from $750,000 to $900,000 if adult education is kept. Easy decision, yes? Cut adult education, yes?

This is the moment to consider the ethic of critique, to be mindful of the "barriers of fairness… . [and investigate] how rules [possibly the college's own practices] have served to disaffect and disadvantage [among others] … low income communities" like those served by adult education (Wood & Hilton, 2012, p. 202). In this scenario, there are no other local providers of adult education.

Of course, this example presents only the smallest sliver of the invaluable information that would be generated through McPhail and McPhail's framework. Even so, in fact, adult education programs are often the first to be cut because they are associated with the community education mission, an early critical mission to be cut, and because they are typically grant funded, they are presumed peripheral to the college's mission. Pausing to consider the ethic of critique helps frame adult education as critical to the college's core mission of providing access for populations most in need of a community college education. Eliminating adult education, therefore, conflicts with a deep-seated view of what is most valued at the college.

Second, does the leadership team cut the high-cost industrial maintenance program? Most general education faculty are hard pressed to embrace the value of such a program, especially if they see retaining it may result in tightened class schedules, meaning they would teach fewer of their favorite 200-level classes, let alone if full-time general education faculty may lose their jobs. This is the moment to consider the ethic of local community, whereby "chief concern is given to local needs (i.e., social, cultural, and economic), workforce development, as well as the advancement of human and intellectual capital" (Wood & Hilton, 2012, p. 207).

In this scenario, manufacturers do not have other colleges to train their critical workforce, and these manufacturers provide good twenty-first-century jobs for local men and women. Again, this example presents only skeletal information, but pausing to consider the ethic of local community helps frame the industrial maintenance program as critical to the college's core mission of meeting community economic needs.

Of note, of course, is this dilemma: the proposal that the two programs in this scenario should be saved seemingly undermines the legitimacy of the strategic planning process because the goal of strategic planning is to realign institutional resources, in particular human resources, in a calculated manner to change the college. Resources cannot be realigned if hard decisions like closing adult education and manufacturing programs are avoided.

Yes, the examples of saving these programs because of their value when examined through ethical lenses challenge leaders to look beyond what may seem most obvious: to return to core institutional values and to have these values play a significant role in strategic planning. Even so, the $750,000 to $900,000 in cuts from the scenario remain. Where does leadership turn when every considered cut will be argued? Only hard decisions remain.

Although every college is different, our experiences are that colleges can decrease operational and personnel costs, for example, by reducing associate-degree majors; by creating a dramatically more efficient course schedule through reducing sections generally and 200-level transfer sections specifically; by creating an affordable staffing plan and realizing this plan through a hiring freeze; by closing low-wage technical programs that have nominal community support; and by holding all faculty and staff to high standards, which, accordingly, means low achievers need to exit the college, even if doing so means closing programs where weak faculty performance condemns the program to poor outcomes. Leaders also must become more entrepreneurial to develop alternate revenue sources, most importantly through the college's foundation where loss-leader investments may be needed.

Acting Decisively

With evidence-based mission priorities established, which include addressing fiscal realities like the $750,000 deficit in the previous scenario, the final point in McPhail and McPhail's strategic planning framework is developing the implementation and results management plan. Its development is akin to the denouement in a work of fiction: it is the wrapping up of loose ends after the plot's climax; it is the proverbial dotting of the i's and crossing of the t's. It is also when the good work of identifying functional leaders and getting their support, giving voice, and reflecting on core institutional values can be lost if leaders do not act decisively. The plague of institutional inertia will fight change even after evidence-based mission priorities have been established and the implementation and results management plan is being written. Well meaning, and not so well meaning, college and community members will create roadblocks to change and will attack supporters of change. They will argue the process was inadequate and will express genuine surprise the college is changing as a result of the newly formed priorities. Hesitation to implement these priorities will embolden critics and will disillusion supporters who had suspended their cynicism about strategic planning.

No, this is not the and-they-all-lived-happily-ever-after point of the strategic planning process. It is the point when leadership is most critical. "The highest expression of leadership," assert Zenger and Folkman (2009), "involves change . . . . leaders are demanded if the organization is to pursue a new path or rise to a significantly higher level of performance" (p. 14).

Leaders who have successfully guided their institutions to this point in the strategic planning process may be confident in the authentic and thoughtful nature of the process. Although always open to new information, especially that indicting unintended consequences, leaders must remain champions of this process by acting resolutely to make real each critical mission-balancing decision.

Boggs and McPhail (2016) argue, "Leaders interested in facilitating organizational change must understand the critical link between the employee's pride in the institution and willingness to support organizational change" (p. 144). The strategic planning process, as described, will have generated this link for many involved because of the role they played in balancing critical missions and evolving the college culture.

References

Boggs, G. R., & McPhail, C. J. (2016). *Practical leadership in community colleges: Navigating today's challenges.* Hoboken, NJ: John Wiley & Sons, Inc.

Llopis, G. (2013, May 20). 6 ways effective listening can make you a better leader. *Forbes.* Retrieved from http://www.forbes.com/sites/glennllopis/2013/05/20/6-effective-ways-listening-can-make-you-a-better-leader/#30933429bf6c

Lunenburg, F. (2010). Formal communication channels: Upward, downward, horizontal, and external. *Focus on Colleges, Universities, and Schools, 4*(1), 1–7.

McPhail, C. J., & McPhail, I. P. (2006). Prioritizing community college missions: A directional effort. In B. K. Townsend & K. J. Dougherty (Eds.), *New Directions for Community Colleges: No. 136. Community college missions in the 21st century* (pp. 91–99). San Francisco, CA: Jossey-Bass.

Wood, J. L., & Hilton, A. A. (2012). Five ethical paradigms for community college leaders: Toward constructing and considering alternative courses of action in ethical decision making. *Community College Review, 40*(3), 196–214.

Zenger, J. H., & Folkman, J. R. (2009). *The extraordinary leader: Turning good managers into great leaders* (2nd ed.). New York, NY: McGraw Hill.

DAVID M. HELLMICH *is president of Sauk Valley Community College in Illinois; he served 28 years as an English professor and administrator at community colleges in Florida, Minnesota, and Kentucky.*

GREG J. FEENEY *is vice president of academics and workforce development and professor of communication at Bluegrass Community and Technical College in Kentucky; his specializations include interpersonal and organizational communication.*

NEW DIRECTIONS FOR COMMUNITY COLLEGES • DOI: 10.1002/cc

10

This chapter highlights key ideas about multiple and competing community college missions and the leadership required to address them.

Making Sense of Multiple Missions

Marilyn J. Amey

Since their inception, community colleges have served multiple roles in the spectrum of U.S. postsecondary education. As the chapters in the volume make clear, the missions of these institutions have not only become greater in number but more complex and more important to achieving the national goal of a more educated populace. Underlying the authors' specific chapter foci are the points that bookend this volume: Community colleges have an implied social contract with the public to act as "the people's college," serving whatever are the local and perhaps regional needs, and fulfilling this contract requires deeply understanding each individual college's mission(s) and enacting it strategically. Although perhaps not signaling a radically new positioning for community college leaders, how to accomplish these directives is no longer obvious—if in fact, it ever really was.

Each chapter in this volume makes clear the competing missions and core values community college leaders are charged to uphold. The chapters thoughtfully lay out the changing nature of what we have long believed are the roles of community colleges: educating students who are increasingly diverse in their preparation and academic goals; hiring faculty prepared to teach across an ever broadening range of learner needs; maintaining low tuition while confronting declining state appropriations, greater restrictions on financial aid for students, deferred maintenance needs and infrastructure updates, and the costs associated with offering baccalaureate degrees; creating and sustaining effective partnerships to offer developmental and concurrent educational opportunities in the face of increased challenges in secondary schools; determining metrics that accurately represent student mobility and academic attainment in ways that appease public officials and accrediting agencies; developing increasing facility to quickly train and retrain for a twenty-first-century workforce; and claiming their place in the national discourse of educational attainment with other public universities and for-profit institutions competing for the same political and economic

New Directions for Community Colleges, no. 180, Winter 2017 © 2017 Wiley Periodicals, Inc.
Published online in Wiley Online Library (wileyonlinelibrary.com) • DOI: 10.1002/cc.20285

stake of higher education writ large. One is left to wonder whether it is possible to maintain this plethora of institutional goals with reasonable success or whether the days of being all things to all people have passed.

Throughout the volume, authors make clear the extent to which the external environment continues to press against the internal values of community colleges as providing a first opportunity for high-quality postsecondary education for historically underserved and less well prepared students, those looking for retooling and workforce preparation, those geographically marginalized from educational opportunities, and those for whom a linear path to academic success has not been clear. Each of the chapter authors lays out key issues associated with their specific mission component, drawing on current research, policy, and practice to showcase ways in which the mission is manifested within a given college or state setting. As important to the volume's purpose, authors raise important questions that must be addressed in order to navigate the complexity of different institutional missions, including deciding to choose between competing missions or to strive to maintain a more comprehensive mission.

Whether it is associated with developmental and adult education, certificates and associate degrees, concurrent enrollment or traditional transfer pathways, the swirl caused by changing expectations, federal and state legislation and policies such as common core, who receives credit and income for student credit hours, when and for what financial aid is available heightens the focus on local arrangements between partners while belying more generalized assessments of accountability. Options heralded as innovative and forward looking such as offering baccalaureates and internationalizing college campuses may enhance student experiences while drawing resources away from the traditional supports offered students that made community colleges distinctive learning environments. Similarly, the rhetoric of free tuition challenges the fact that different forms and incentives for this initiative do not have the same outcomes across the board for students or for colleges. The complex relationship between cost, access, retention and goal achievement, and public perception has to be clearly addressed before such policies benefit more than they confound the colleges' ability to achieve its many missions. How college leaders navigate and establish effective pathways for students to achieve academic learning objectives while simultaneously meeting institutional goals is politically charged and likely to continue being turbulent as education policies evolve in the future. Resolving these challenges and determining relevant institutional choices may require limiting curricular offerings at times, focusing energies in certain more sustainable directions, or forming distinctive institutional consortia, again changing the ways in which community colleges respond to the constituent needs.

In different ways, Mellow and Heelan, Ayers, and Hellmich and Feeney suggest that without strategic thinking, the education social contract is threatened, and colleges are left to react and chase their purpose(s) rather than strategically plan for and decide among the options. As senior administrators and other policy and decision makers address the complex realities that confront them, this volume makes clear that community college leadership has never been more important. The myriad areas of the college that most clearly are charged with aspects of the multiple missions described in this volume need to be brought to the table to be involved with strategic planning. Generating commitment and ensuring these key voices are at the table builds capacity throughout the college, which might be one of the most important yet often untapped resources. This likely requires questioning the college's objectives in its current and future community context. How to prioritize cannot be just what has historically been; at the same time, when needing to cull programs or traditional initiatives, how deep the consequences run and for whom has to be taken into account.

In sum, determining how to grow, how to reach diverse and increasing numbers of students, how to be relevant, and how to provide the financial foundation for these decisions are all important questions to meeting the future missions of the community college. Leadership is necessary at all levels to make the critical and decisive decisions that drive the future mission(s) of the community college.

MARILYN J. AMEY *is professor of higher, adult, and lifelong education and chairperson of the department of Educational Administration at Michigan State University.*

NEW DIRECTIONS FOR COMMUNITY COLLEGES • DOI: 10.1002/cc

INDEX

NEW DIRECTIONS FOR COMMUNITY COLLEGE
ORDER FORM SUBSCRIPTION AND SINGLE ISSUES

DISCOUNTED BACK ISSUES:

Use this form to receive 20% off all back issues of *New Directions for Community College*.
All single issues priced at **$23.20** (normally $29.00)

TITLE	ISSUE NO.	ISBN
_____	_____	_____
_____	_____	_____
_____	_____	_____

Call 1-800-835-6770 or see mailing instructions below. When calling, mention the promotional code JBNND to receive your discount. For a complete list of issues, please visit www.wiley.com/WileyCDA/WileyTitle/productCd-CC.html

SUBSCRIPTIONS: (1 YEAR, 4 ISSUES)

☐ New Order   ☐ Renewal

U.S.	☐ Individual: $89	☐ Institutional: $356
Canada/Mexico	☐ Individual: $89	☐ Institutional: $398
All Others	☐ Individual: $113	☐ Institutional: $434

Call 1-800-835-6770 or see mailing and pricing instructions below.
Online subscriptions are available at www.onlinelibrary.wiley.com

ORDER TOTALS:

Issue / Subscription Amount: $ _____

Shipping Amount: $ _____
(for single issues only – subscription prices include shipping)

Total Amount: $ _____

SHIPPING CHARGES:
First Item $6.00
Each Add'l Item $2.00

(No sales tax for U.S. subscriptions. Canadian residents, add GST for subscription orders. Individual rate subscriptions must be paid by personal check or credit card. Individual rate subscriptions may not be resold as library copies.)

BILLING & SHIPPING INFORMATION:

☐ **PAYMENT ENCLOSED:** *(U.S. check or money order only. All payments must be in U.S. dollars.)*

☐ **CREDIT CARD:** ☐ VISA   ☐ MC   ☐ AMEX

Card number _____Exp. Date_____

Card Holder Name_____Card Issue # _____

Signature _____Day Phone_____

☐ **BILL ME:** *(U.S. institutional orders only. Purchase order required.)*

Purchase order # _____
Federal Tax ID 13559302 • GST 89102-8052

Name_____

Address_____

Phone_____ E-mail_____

Copy or detach page and send to: **John Wiley & Sons, Inc. / Jossey Bass**
PO Box 55381
Boston, MA 02205-9850

PROMO JBNND